Editorial Project Manager
Eric Migliaccio

Editor in Chief
Karen J. Goldfluss, M.S. Ed.

Creative Director
Sarah M. Fournier

Cover Artist
Barb Lorseyedi

Illustrator
Clint McKnight

Art Coordinator
Renée Mc Elwee

Imaging
Amanda R. Harter

Publisher
Mary D. Smith, M.S. Ed.

Author

Janna Anderson, M.A.

For correlations to the Common Core State Standards, see pages 94–96 of this book or visit *http://www.teachercreated.com/standards/*.

Teacher Created Resources
6421 Industry Way
Westminster, CA 92683
www.teachercreated.com
ISBN: 978-1-4206-3544-7

© 2015 Teacher Created Resources
Made in U.S.A.

TABLE OF CONTENTS

Counting by 7s by Holly Goldberg Sloan

All the Broken Pieces by Ann E. Burg

Section I: Using the Novels Together

Unit 1: Characterization

Individual: "Getting to Know the Characters" — *Collaborative:* "Comparing Protagonists" — *Individual:* "Chosen Family" — *Individual:* "Thanks for the Support" — *Individual:* "More Than a Label" — *Collaborative:* "Discussing Labels"

Unit 2: Plot

Collaborative: "Story Sequence" — *Individual:* "Types of Conflict" — *Collaborative:* "Taking the Conflict Further" — *Collaborative:* "Plotting Problems" — *Individual:* "Turning Points" — *Collaborative:* "Talking About Turning Points" — *Individual:* "Resolution"

Unit 3: Setting and Genre

Individual: "Genre Comparison: Past and Present" — *Collaborative:* "Connecting History to the Present" — *Collaborative:* "Location, Location!" — *Individual:* "A Sense of Place" — *Collaborative:* "Setting and Meaning"

Unit 4: Theme

Collaborative: "Theme Seeds" — *Individual:* "Lending Their Support" — *Collaborative:* "Feeling Broken" — *Individual:* "Taking the Analysis Further" — *Individual:* "Becoming Part of a Team" — *Individual:* "Family Matters" — *Individual Essay Assignment:* "Comparing a Theme"

CONNECTING WITH THE COMMON CORE

This book responds to the Common Core State Standards' goals of helping students develop the skills necessary to be successful in college and career. Through focused analysis, comparison, and synthesis of two texts, students will strengthen their understanding of literary conventions and build on analytical and argumentation skills. The texts selected for this book represent the high-quality, complex, and engaging new literature that is being produced in today's middle-grade publishing. These contemporary titles are easily relatable to the 21st-century child's experiences and knowledge, creating deeper connections between reader and text and giving the young reader a sense of ownership over the material.

The Common Core State Standards call for emphasis on assignments that encourage students to think critically, analyze deeply, and cite extensively from texts. Under the Common Core Standards, students are expected to progress in their level of comprehension and acquire appropriate academic vocabulary. In addition to building their reading and writing skills, students must also develop their listening and speaking skills in ways that will prepare them for the academic rigor of college.

To increase college readiness, Language Arts assignments are moving away from personal response and toward critical analysis based on information from texts. To prepare for the work they will encounter in college, students must become skilled at developing a strong claim and defending it with evidence from texts. To that end, *Using Paired Novels to Build Close Reading Skills* provides students with opportunities to interact with reading material deeply and in a variety of ways. Comparison activities strengthen students' understanding of the novels themselves, as well as the craft of writing. These

> The activities in this resource focus on two specific novels— *Counting by 7s* and *All the Broken Pieces*—but this same approach can be similarly applied when analyzing and comparing literature in general.

activities prompt students to examine how each author approaches literary elements such as characterization, theme, and point of view, and to draw conclusions based on the similarities or differences. In order to complete the tasks in these activities, students will need to reflect on their understanding of one book before making connections to the other—a process that will naturally support comprehension skills. The activities in this resource focus on two specific novels—*Counting by 7s* and *All the Broken Pieces*—but this same approach can be similarly applied when analyzing and comparing literature in general.

The activities in this book provide opportunities for individual and collaborative experiences. The individual activities build reading and writing skills by prompting students to develop analytical arguments and cite evidence from the texts. The collaborative activities help students develop critical speaking and listening skills in the context of literary analysis.

Ultimately, we want our children to develop a love of books and to become life-long readers. They can and should be encouraged to make personal connections to the texts and express their feelings about the stories they read. In fact, these types of connections often form the starting point for activities with more academic rigor. To provide students with freedom to interact with texts in more personal and creative ways, we have included Interactive Literature Notebook assignments as well as creative collaborative activities that are intended to enrich the reading experience and foster deeper personal enjoyment of the novels while still providing the foundation for deeper critical engagement.

HOW TO USE THIS BOOK

Section I (Units 1–5)

The purpose of this book is to provide you with a variety of activities that connect the two novels in ways that will foster deeper critical and analytical thinking in your students. Section I contains worksheets to be completed after both novels have been read. This section is divided into five units, which are based on the following literary elements: **Characterization** (pages 8–15), **Plot** (pages 16–25), **Setting and Genre** (pages 26–32), **Theme** (pages 33–49), and **Craft and Structure** (pages 50–61).

Unit features include . . .

✳ Teacher Instructions

The first page of each unit provides you with an overview of the concept, the relevance to student learning, and brief descriptions and suggestions for each activity in the unit.

✳ Quick Guide to the Concept

The top portion of this page provides your students with an introduction to the literary concept around which the unit is built, along with a list of related vocabulary words. The bottom portion contains a list of suggestions for **Interactive Literature Notebook** entries. The Interactive Literature Notebook can be used to allow students to think creatively about the reading and make personal connections to the novels. Some of the ideas can apply to both books, while others are specific to one or the other novel. You can assign a specific topic to your students or allow them to pick from these suggestions. More detailed instructions for the Interactive Literature Notebook can be found on page 6.

✳ Unit Activities

Each unit contains **individual** and **collaborative** activities that support your students' understanding of literary elements and author's craft. Most of the activities also emphasize the use of textual evidence in the form of summarizing, paraphrasing, or quoting. In addition, some are meant to be used as **linked** assignments, with one activity laying the foundation for the next. In some cases, a collaborative activity allows students to brainstorm ideas and discuss the books together before completing a more challenging task in an individual worksheet. Alternately, an individual activity may provide students with an opportunity to reflect on the reading and then practice listening, speaking, and paraphrasing skills in a linked collaborative activity. Look for the following icons in the upper-right corner of each activity page:

 = individual   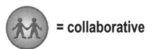 = collaborative   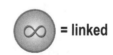 = linked

Section II (Units 6–8)

In this section, you will find activities to use during the reading of the individual books. These activities are divided into three groups: those that can be used with either novel, those intended to be used with *Counting by 7s,* and those intended to be used with *All the Broken Pieces.* These activities are meant to supplement the single-novel study activities you may already use. You may want to have students keep all of their single-novel worksheets in a folder and refer back to them when they are completing the novel-comparison activities. This will provide your students with opportunities to review the material, refresh their memories of the books, and practice using notes as a reference for a current assignment.

WHAT IS AN INTERACTIVE LITERATURE NOTEBOOK?

An Interactive Literature Notebook is a notebook that combines learning materials with personal response. For each student, his or her notebook will serve as a place to record and organize the information learned about the elements of literature. The response pages also encourage a deeper level of creativity and personal reflection toward the novels being analyzed and discussed in class.

For this resource, students may use a composition book, a spiral notebook, or a three-ring binder, depending on teacher preferences and needs. Instruct students to organize their notebooks as follows:

On the RIGHT side of the notebook: Students record new information they are learning about literary elements and writer's craft.

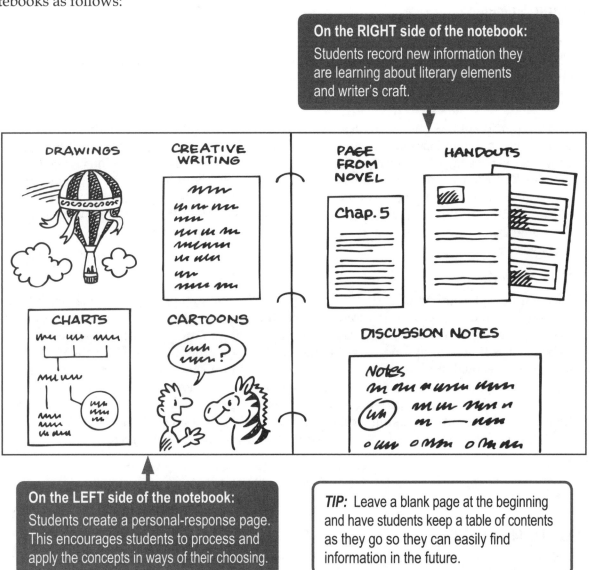

On the LEFT side of the notebook: Students create a personal-response page. This encourages students to process and apply the concepts in ways of their choosing.

TIP: Leave a blank page at the beginning and have students keep a table of contents as they go so they can easily find information in the future.

Interactive Literature Notebooks help your students hone the organizational skills they will need to be successful learners in high school and college by developing their competence in note-taking and record-keeping. These notebooks are excellent tools for visual as well as linguistic learners, and they give all students experience in connecting visual and multimedia components with text.

CONTEMPORARY CLASSICS

Counting by 7s

Holly Goldberg Sloan (2013)

In this touching novel, 12-year-old Willow is devastated by the sudden loss of her adoptive parents, but she finds love, support, and acceptance in a group of virtual strangers who come together to help her. Willow, who has always felt like an outsider, is a genius with an unusual way of viewing the world. The novel's secondary characters are equally interesting and well developed, and each makes a unique and important contribution to Willow's growth.

First-person narration captures Willow's unconventional take on the world, as well as the depth of emotion she experiences during tragedy. The author also intersperses chapters written in third-person to give readers insight into the secondary characters and events happening outside Willow's experience. Readers will connect with the story's themes of supportive friendships, acceptance, perseverance, and new beginnings.

Awards and Honors

- ➤ *New York Times* Best Seller
- ➤ An Amazon Best Book of the Year 2013
- ➤ B.E.A. Buzz Book Award 2013
- ➤ A *School Library Journal* Best Book of the Year 2013
- ➤ Dorothy Canfield Fisher Children's Book Award Nominee 2014–2015

Note: Page numbers in this guide refer to the 2014 paperback edition published by Puffin Books, Penguin Young Readers Group, New York.

All the Broken Pieces

Ann E. Burg (2009)

All the Broken Pieces is a work of historical fiction told through free-verse poetry. Matt is a young boy who came to the U.S. as a refugee at the end of the Vietnam War. Although he now has a loving and supportive adoptive family, Matt is haunted by memories of the family and home he has lost, as well as the violence he witnessed. He faces prejudice and resentment but also finds love, support, and understanding that help him work toward overcoming tragedy.

This fast-paced and memorable novel provides an opportunity for learning about the impact of the Vietnam War on veterans, families, refugees, and those left behind in Vietnam. The first-person narration along with the poetic form gives readers insight into the emotions and thoughts of a refugee of war. Burg explores the transformative power of opening up to others.

Awards and Honors

- ➤ ALA Best Books for Young Adults 2010
- ➤ Booklist Top Ten First Novels for Youth 2009
- ➤ Booklist Top Ten Historical Fiction for Youth 2009
- ➤ Cybil's Awards Finalist 2009
- ➤ Winner of the 2010 Jefferson Cup

Note: Page numbers in this guide refer to the 2009 paperback edition published by Scholastic, Inc., New York.

UNIT 1 TEACHER INSTRUCTIONS

When students analyze *character*, they increase their comprehension of the author's craft and purpose, and they build their understanding of the way character development relates to theme. In this unit, your class will analyze how the authors of *Counting by 7s* and *All the Broken Pieces* reveal levels of the protagonists (main characters) and how the secondary characters contribute to each story. Students will make connections between the characters in these two novels, discuss and write about the ways the protagonists respond to challenges, and draw conclusions based on evidence from the text.

Introduce students to the concept of characterization by distributing the top portion of "A Quick Guide to Characterization" (page 9). The bottom portion offers suggestions for using Interactive Notebooks to reinforce learning. Distribute any or all of these when appropriate.

Unit 1 includes the following components. See page 5 of this book for an explanation of icons.

"Getting to Know the Characters" (page 10) — Consider author's craft and examine the ways in which authors develop characters. Examine how the protagonists view themselves, how they act, and how others view them in the novel, as well as how they change.

"Comparing Protagonists" (page 11) — Build both discussion and collaboration skills by brainstorming a list of traits for each main character and drawing conclusions about the characters' similarities.

"Chosen Family" (page 12) — After engaging in close readings of two passages, draw conclusions about the ways each character differs in response to his or her adoption.

"Thanks for the Support" (page 13) — Consider the roles of secondary characters in the novels and decide which character in each novel is most influential in supporting the novel's main character. Provide evidence to support opinions.

"More Than a Label" (page 14) — Read passages from one novel and apply the concept of labeling to characters in both novels.

"Discussing Labels" (page 15) — Work together to consider more positive ways to label people. Then take turns answering questions and summarizing partners' claims.

A QUICK GUIDE TO CHARACTERIZATION

Great stories need great *characters*. Characters are the people or animals in a story. The author helps us get to know the characters through *characterization*. This is the process of giving readers clues that help us understand who the characters are and why they are important to the story.

* What does the character say?
* How does the character act?
* What does the character look like?
* What do other characters say about him or her?
* How do other characters react to him or her?

The *protagonist* is the main character of the story.

The *antagonist* is the person or force that is against the main character.

Secondary characters are characters who are important but are not the main focus of the story. They help move the plot along and help us understand the main character.

A character that changes by the end of the novel is called a *dynamic* character.

Characters that stay the same throughout the novel are called *static* characters.

Unit Vocabulary
- ✓ characters
- ✓ characterization
- ✓ protagonist
- ✓ antagonist
- ✓ secondary characters
- ✓ dynamic character
- ✓ static character

INTERACTIVE LITERATURE NOTEBOOK SUGGESTIONS FOR UNIT 1

1 Character Collage	2 Growing and Changing	3 Compared to Me	4 My Mentor	5 An Act of Love	6 Homework Assignment
Use pictures and words to create a character collage that represents the protagonist of one of the novels. In the middle of the page, write down a quote that represents the main character.	After reading a few chapters of the novel, stop and think about the main character. How do you think that character will change by the end of the book? Why do you think this?	In *Counting by 7s*, there are several interesting and unique characters. Which character in the novel is most like you? Which one is least like you? Create a chart in which you compare yourself to one or more characters.	Describe a teacher, coach, or other older person who has been a mentor to you. How has this person influenced you?	In *All the Broken Pieces*, Matt worries that his real mother gave him away because she didn't love him. Write a letter to Matt from his mother explaining why this was an act of love.	In *All the Broken Pieces*, the poem on page 58 describes Matt's homework assignment to write a short character sketch of someone he knows. Read this poem and do the assignment for someone in your life.

Name: _____

GETTING TO KNOW THE CHARACTERS

Look closely at how the authors help us get to know the main characters. Use evidence from the novels to support your answers.

	Willow	Matt
How do the protagonists describe themselves?		
Quotation to support answer		
How do the protagonists act at the beginning of the novel?		
Quotation to support answer		
How do other characters view the protagonists at the beginning?		
Quotation to support answer		
How do the protagonists act at the end of the novel?		
Quotation to support answer		
How do other people view them at the end?		
Quotation to support answer		

Name(s): _____

COMPARING PROTAGONISTS

With a partner or in a small group, brainstorm a list of traits that describe the protagonist of each novel. Discuss which traits they have in common. As a group, decide which traits are most important and why.

Words that describe Willow   **Words that describe both**   **Words that describe Matt**

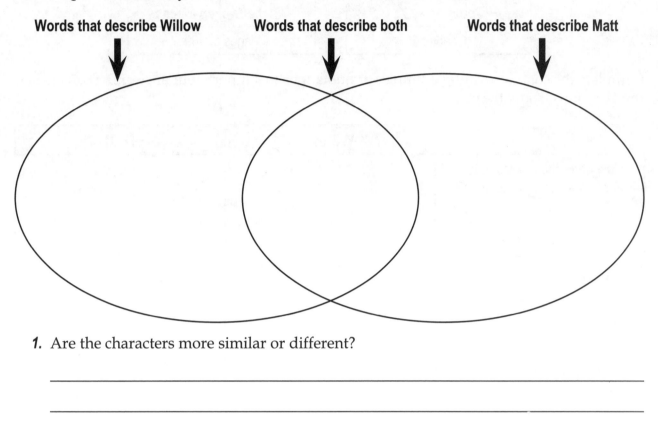

1. Are the characters more similar or different?

_____

_____

_____

2. Which personality trait or characteristic does your group think stands out the most in each character?

	Willow	**Matt**
Trait or characteristic		
How is this trait important to the story?		
Is this also an important trait for the character in the other novel?		
Explain why or why not.		

Name: _____

CHOSEN FAMILY

Matt and Willow are both adopted by loving parents, but they express different feelings about their family situations. Read the following passages:

Counting by 7s
Chapter 2

All the Broken Pieces
pages 63–69

Complete the chart, providing examples or quotations to support your answers. Then answer the questions below the chart.

	Willow	**Matt**
How does the character feel about the adoptive parents?		
Evidence that supports your answer		
How do the parents seem to feel about their adopted child?		
Evidence that supports your answer		

1. How are Matt's feelings and concerns about his parents different from Willow's?

_____

_____

_____

2. Why do you think Matt feels this way but Willow does not?

_____

_____

_____

UNIT 1: CHARACTERIZATION

Name: _____

THANKS FOR THE SUPPORT

Think about the *secondary* or *supporting characters* in each story and how they influence Willow and Matt. Consider the following characters:

Counting by 7s
Dell Duke
Mai
Pattie
Jairo

All the Broken Pieces
Jeff
Coach Robeson
Chris
Caveman Joe

All of these characters are important in the novels. Which one from each novel do you think was the most important in helping the protagonist overcome the conflict, grow, and change?

Willow was most influenced by _____

because _____

_____

_____

Quotation: _____

_____

Page number: _____

Matt was most influenced by _____

because _____

_____

_____

Quotation: _____

_____

Page number: _____

Are the two characters you picked more similar or different? Explain.

_____

_____

_____

Name: _____

MORE THAN A LABEL

In *Counting by 7s*, Dell Duke creates his "System of the Strange" to help him categorize students and make his job easier, and he eventually adds categories for Pattie Nguyen and himself. Read the scene (Chapter 58, pages 358–359) in which Willow discovers Dell's system and reacts to it.

1. At first, Willow is disturbed by the list when she finds it. After thinking about Dell and his system, what does Willow realize he was trying to do?

_____

_____

2. What does Willow say she has learned about labels?

_____

_____

3. In *All the Broken Pieces*, Matt is very troubled. If he had been sent to see Dell Duke, which category do you think Dell would have placed him in? Explain why.

_____

_____

_____

Select two other characters from *Counting by 7s* and two characters from *All the Broken Pieces*. Show how each character demonstrates characteristics of at least two of Dell's categories. See *Counting by 7s* (Chapter 5, pages 44–45) for definitions of the first four categories.

Character	Categories	How the Character Fits the Categories
	1. 2.	
	1. 2.	
	1. 2.	
	1. 2.	

14

Name(s): _____

DISCUSSING LABELS

Share your answers from the worksheet "More Than a Label" (page 14) before completing this worksheet.

After sharing your answers from your character charts with each other, select one character from each book. Decide on a new *positive* label that also fits this character.

Character: _____ **From:** _____ *Counting by 7s* _____

New Positive Label: _____

Explanation: _____

_____

_____

_____

Character: _____ **From:** _____ *All the Broken Pieces* _____

New Positive Label: _____

Explanation: _____

_____

_____

_____

PRACTICE SPEAKING AND LISTENING!

Speaker 1: _____
(name)

Speaker 2: _____
(name)

Answer the following question aloud and support your opinion with examples from the novels.

How can labeling <u>other people</u> cause problems?

Listen to Speaker 1's answer. Use your own words to summarize your partner's claim.

then

Answer the following question aloud and support your opinion with examples from the novels.

How can labeling <u>yourself</u> cause problems?

Listen to Speaker 2's answer. Use your own words to summarize your partner's claim.

UNIT 2 TEACHER INSTRUCTIONS

The *plot* is the series of events that make up the action of the novel. It is what *happens* in the story. The *conflict*, the problem at the heart of the story, is an essential part of the plot. A chronological plot describes events in the order they happen and usually follows a traditional structure: Exposition, Rising Action, Climax, Falling Action, and Resolution.

In this unit, students will analyze plot structure, conflict, and resolution. They will compare how the characters deal with conflicts, and they will draw conclusions about the similarities and differences in the plots of these novels. Students will use critical and creative thinking to articulate their understanding of plot structure.

Introduce students to the concept of plot by distributing the top portion of "A Quick Guide to Plot" (page 17) and "A Quick Guide to Plot Structure" (page 18). The bottom portion of page 17 offers suggestions for using Interactive Notebooks to reinforce learning. Distribute any or all of these when appropriate.

Unit 2 includes the following components. See page 5 of this book for an explanation of icons.

 "Story Sequence" (page 19) — Work together to determine the major plot points in each novel, dividing them into "Beginning," "Middle," and "End." Groups then examine the similarities and differences in the novels' plots.

 "Types of Conflict" (page 20) — Consider how three common types of conflict appear in each novel.

 "Taking the Conflict Further" (page 21) — Build on the ideas generated in the "Types of Conflict" worksheet. In groups of three to four members, share ideas and discuss the most significant type of conflict in the novels.

 "Plotting Problems" (page 22) — Identify three significant plot points that help the characters grow. After identifying examples of major struggles in each novel, discuss the similarities and differences in the ways the characters respond to conflict.

 "Turning Points" (page 23) — Read significant sections of the books to understand how major plot points affect the story as a whole. (*TIP:* Consider reading these sections aloud and having students summarize afterwards.)

 "Talking About Turning Points" (page 24) — Practice listening and speaking by taking notes on each other's summaries and furthering the discussion.

 "Resolution" (page 25) — Examine the resolution to each novel, summarize, make comparisons, and draw conclusions.

A QUICK GUIDE TO PLOT

The *plot* is what happens in the story. It is made up of the events that take place in a specific *sequence* in the book, from the **beginning** to the **middle** to the **end**.

The *conflict* is the main problem in the story. There are several types of conflicts, including the following:

Unit Vocabulary
- ✓ plot
- ✓ sequence
- ✓ conflict
- ✓ exposition
- ✓ climax
- ✓ resolution

* **Person vs. Person** – The main character struggles with another person or people in the story.

* **Person vs. Self** – The main character struggles with emotions, thoughts, or feelings that create the problems in the story.

* **Person vs. Nature** – The main character struggles with something in nature, such as the wilderness or a big storm.

* **Person vs. Society** – The main character struggles against the beliefs, behaviors, or traditions of society.

INTERACTIVE LITERATURE NOTEBOOK SUGGESTIONS FOR UNIT 2

1 What Happens Next?	2 Filmstrip	3 An Important Scene	4 A New Place	5 Tweet It!
Predict the fictional future: based on the events in the story, what do you think will happen next? What will happen five years after the story ends? Write a paragraph in which you imagine the future events for these characters.	Create a filmstrip of several major events in the story.	Find or create pictures that represent one of the most important scenes in the story. Write a summary of the scene and an explanation about why you chose it.	If you have ever moved to a new place, write about your experience. Even if you did not move to a new country, what changes did you have to adjust to?	In 140 characters or fewer, explain what this book is about.

A QUICK GUIDE TO PLOT STRUCTURE

Many novels follow a classic plot structure. They first introduce characters, and then they introduce conflict into the lives of those characters. Characters struggle with this conflict (or conflicts) until a turning point occurs. By the end of the novel, this conflict is resolved.

The following diagram shows this structure. Each point on the diagram is explained below.

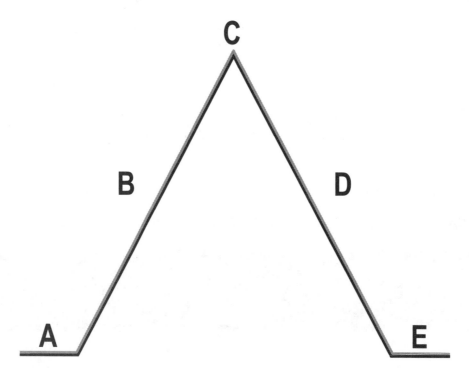

A. **Exposition** – the information and events that set up the story and introduce characters

B. **Rising Action** – the series of events that build excitement or tension by showing the characters struggling with the conflict

C. **Climax** – the most tense or exciting part of the story and the turning point when we begin to see how the conflict might end

D. **Falling Action** – the events that show what happens to the characters after the conflict is resolved or is beginning to be resolved

E. **Resolution** – the ending

Name(s): _____

STORY SEQUENCE

Work together to complete the following charts before answering the questions below.

➤ **Chart 1:** Brainstorm a list of the most important events in each section of the novels.

➤ **Chart 2:** Make a list of the similarities and the differences in the plots of the novels.

Chart 1	*Counting by 7s*	*All the Broken Pieces*
Beginning		
Middle		
End		

Chart 2	**Similarities in Plots**	**Differences in Plots**

1. What is the most significant similarity? Why?

_____

_____

_____

2. What is the most significant difference? Why?

_____

_____

_____

Name: _____

TYPES OF CONFLICT

The conflict of the story is the problem the main character faces. Most stories have more than one type of conflict. Complete the chart to show how three different types of conflict are presented in the novels.

	Person vs. Society How do attitudes or behaviors of the culture and/or government cause conflict for the main characters?	Person vs. Person How does the protagonist struggle against another character or characters in the novel?	Person vs. Self What thoughts, behaviors, or emotions does the main character struggle to overcome?
Counting by 7s			
Quotation that shows this conflict:			
Page number(s):			
All the Broken Pieces			
Quotation that shows this conflict:			
Page number(s):			

     20   ©Teacher Created Resources

Name(s): _____

TAKING THE CONFLICT FURTHER

With your group, share your chart from the "Types of Conflict" worksheet. Each person in the group should share at least one conflict and example. When one person is talking, the rest of the group should listen carefully.

1. Were your group members' answers more similar or different?

	More Similar	More Different
Counting by 7s		
➤ Person vs. Society	◯	◯
➤ Person vs. Person	◯	◯
➤ Person vs. Self	◯	◯
All the Broken Pieces		
➤ Person vs. Society	◯	◯
➤ Person vs. Person	◯	◯
➤ Person vs. Self	◯	◯

2. Which type of conflict does your group think is the most important conflict for Willow?

_____

Why? _____

_____

_____

3. Which type of conflict does your group think is the most important conflict for Matt?

_____

Why? _____

_____

_____

4. Did your group pick the same conflict for both answers?   **Yes   No**

Why do you think your answers were the same or different?

_____

_____

_____

Name(s): _____

PLOTTING PROBLEMS

The plots of both novels include many difficult and even traumatic situations Matt and Willow face. How do the characters react to these situations? Think about how these struggles affect the choices the characters make. Find three examples of difficult problems each character faces. Discuss how these characters react to each situation.

	Willow	Matt
Problem #1		
Reaction		
Page numbers		
Problem #2		
Reaction		
Page numbers		
Problem #3		
Reaction		
Page numbers		

Answer the following questions about how these characters react to problems.

1. Explain one way Willow and Matt's reactions to difficult circumstances are similar.

_____

_____

_____

2. Explain one way Willow and Matt respond differently to difficult circumstances.

_____

_____

_____

Name: _____

TURNING POINTS

For each novel, read the passage listed. As you do so, think about how the events in these sections show a shift in each main character's thinking and behavior.

from *Counting by 7s*	from *All the Broken Pieces*
Chapter 46 (pages 279–290)	pages 164–173

Summarize what happened in this chapter.

Summarize what happened in these poems.

In this chapter, find a quotation that shows how Willow is beginning to feel like her old self again.

_____

_____

_____

_____

Page number of quotation: _____

In these poems, find a quotation that shows how Matt feels about the way the kids are treating Chris.

_____

_____

_____

_____

Page number of quotation: _____

Name(s): _____

TALKING ABOUT TURNING POINTS

You have just summarized important scenes in *Counting by 7s* and *All the Broken Pieces*. Work with a partner to discuss your summaries and answer questions about the novels. One partner will read his or her summary for the chapter in *Counting by 7s* while the other partner listens and writes notes. Then you will switch roles for *All the Broken Pieces*.

	Counting by 7s	*All the Broken Pieces*
Speaker's Name		
Listener's Name		
Listener's Notes ➤ **What I liked** ➤ **What is missing** ➤ **What is confusing**		

Now discuss the following questions and write your answers.

1. What is different about the way the protagonist acts in this passage compared to his or her behavior before this event?

   Counting by 7s: _____

   _____

   All the Broken Pieces: _____

   _____

2. In both novels, other people's actions influence the protagonists' behavior. How are the novels similar in this way?

   _____

   _____

   _____

3. How are the novels different in this way?

   _____

   _____

   _____

24

Name: _____

RESOLUTION

The ending of a book should follow logically from the sequence of events in the story. Reread the last chapters of each book and answer the questions below.

	Counting by 7s	All the Broken Pieces
In your own words, explain what happens at the end of the novel.		
Did it end the way you expected it to? Explain why or why not.		
What is your opinion of the way the book ends?		

1. In what ways are the endings similar in these books?

_____

_____

2. In what ways are the endings different?

_____

_____

3. Which ending did you like better?　❑ *Counting by 7s*　❑ *All the Broken Pieces*

4. Explain your answer to question #3.

_____

_____

_____

UNIT 3 TEACHER INSTRUCTIONS

The *setting* of a novel is an important element to examine. Students should be able to identify not just the *time* and *place* of the story, but also how those details influence characters and drive plot. Readers should be asked to examine how the environment affects the people and events in the story. Additionally, students can analyze the writer's craft by identifying how the author uses details and descriptions to create a vivid environment.

Setting is also an essential part of identifying the *genre* of each of these novels: *historical fiction* and *contemporary realistic fiction*. In this unit, students will examine how setting relates to genre in historical and contemporary realistic fiction. By looking closely at how time period affects story and comparing how these different genres are crafted, readers will gain a deeper understanding of differences in genre and its relationship to the writer's purpose.

Introduce students to the concepts of setting and genre by distributing the top portion of "A Quick Guide to Setting and Genre" (page 27). The bottom portion offers suggestions for using Interactive Notebooks to reinforce learning. Distribute any or all of these when appropriate.

Unit 3 includes the following components. See page 5 of this book for an explanation of icons.

"Genre Comparison: Past and Present" (page 28) — Identify details in the stories that relate to the time during which each novel takes place. While doing so, consider the importance of the time period to the plot of each novel.

"Connecting History to the Present" (page 29) — Share work from the previous activity and discuss the importance of real historical events in each novel.

"Location, Location!" (page 30) — Work with a partner to brainstorm lists of the different locations the author introduces in each book. Practice listening, speaking, and summarization skills by taking turns explaining the importance of one location in the books.

"A Sense of Place" (page 31) — Read closely to identify, explain, and compare the authors' use of descriptive words and sensory details to create vivid environments. (*TIP:* Read the passages aloud and have students note examples of sensory details as you read. Ask students to identify which details appeal to which senses.)

"Setting and Meaning" (page 32) — Build collaborative skills by discussing the connections between setting and tone, as well as examining how specific places described in each novel are relevant to the overall story.

A QUICK GUIDE TO SETTING AND GENRE

The *setting* of a book tells the reader **where** and **when** the story takes place and what the *environment* of the story is like. The author uses details and descriptions to help the reader imagine where the characters are. A book may have more than one setting; or there could be one general setting, like a city, and scenes that take place in different locations within that general setting.

Settings can sometimes help us identify the *genre* of the book. A genre—such as like nonfiction, fantasy, or historical fiction—is a type of text. Novels that take place in the past and describe made-up characters in real historical events are in the genre of *historical fiction*. Novels that take place in our time and describe made-up characters and events that could really happen are in the genre called *realistic fiction*.

Unit Vocabulary
- ✓ setting
- ✓ environment
- ✓ genre
- ✓ historical fiction
- ✓ realistic fiction

INTERACTIVE LITERATURE NOTEBOOK SUGGESTIONS FOR UNIT 3

1 Vivid Description	2 Plant Life	3 Timeline	4 The 1970s	5 A Country's Culture	6 About a Sport
The Nguyens' home, the salon, and Dell Duke's apartment are all very important settings in *Counting by 7s*. The author creates vivid descriptions to help readers visualize these places. Select a room in your home and write a vivid description of it.	One of Willow's interests is plants. She had an elaborate garden in her parents' house, and she helps her new friends make their own. Go to a park, arboretum, or your own back yard and observe the plants. Write a detailed description of this place.	Make a timeline of the Vietnam War.	*All the Broken Pieces* takes place in the 1970s. Create a collage of images, facts, and headlines from the '70s.	For the first two years Matt lives in America, he goes to weekly classes to learn about Vietnamese culture. Research Vietnam's culture and create a collage of images and words.	Several scenes in *All the Broken Pieces* describe Matt's practices and baseball games. If you play a sport or attend a sporting event, pay attention to the details you hear, see, smell, touch, and taste. Write a descriptive paragraph of the event. Find images to match your details.

GENRE COMPARISON: PAST AND PRESENT

Counting by 7s and *All the Broken Pieces* share similar themes and topics, but one is historical fiction and one is contemporary fiction because of *when* the stories take place. Novels that take place in the past and portray real historical events in the storytelling are called *historical fiction*. Novels that take place in our current time are called *realistic fiction* or *contemporary realistic fiction*. Think about how each author shows the time period that is part of each book's setting.

All the Broken Pieces

1. When does this novel take place? _____

2. What real historical events are important to the plot and characters in this book?

   _____

   _____

3. How does the author make the time period come alive for the reader?

   _____

   _____

4. Find a quotation that helps you understand the events of this time. Write it here.

   _____

   _____

5. Could Matt's story take place at any time or only during that time? Explain.

   _____

   _____

Counting by 7s

1. When does this novel take place? _____

2. List details that make this story contemporary. What references to current times does the author make, and how do these references help make the story feel contemporary?

   _____

   _____

3. Could Willow's story take place at any time or only during this time? Explain.

   _____

   _____

UNIT 3: SETTING AND GENRE

Name(s): _____

CONNECTING HISTORY TO THE PRESENT

Share your answers from the "Genre Comparison: Past and Present" worksheet. Work together to brainstorm ideas and answer the questions below.

All the Broken Pieces takes place in the past and tells the story of a boy who is a refugee from the Vietnam War. In *Counting by 7s*, Pattie Nguyen is also from Vietnam. Read pages 70–71 (in Chapter 9) from that novel. Based on this passage about Pattie's history, brainstorm a list of similarities and differences between Matt's family history and Pattie's.

Similarities	Differences

1. Reread the stanza on page 161 of *All the Broken Pieces*. Explain what the veteran means when he says what he says about Matt's birth father.

   _____
   _____
   _____

2. Both authors use historically accurate facts to help them create their stories. During the Vietnam War, many American soldiers fathered children with Vietnamese women. Many of these couples considered themselves to be in serious relationships, yet when the soldiers were sent back home, they lost contact with their girlfriends and children. How did Ann Burg use these facts to make *All the Broken Pieces* feel historically accurate?

   _____
   _____
   _____

3. Pattie is not the main character of *Counting by 7s*, so the author does not provide very many details about her history or how she feels about Vietnam, her childhood during the war, or her American father. Did reading *All the Broken Pieces* help you understand Pattie better? Explain.

   _____
   _____
   _____

Name(s): _____

LOCATION, LOCATION!

With a partner, list the different places that are described in each novel. Where does the action take place? Think about big settings, like cities, as well as small settings, like someone's house. Each author describes several places. See how many you can name.

Counting by 7s	All the Broken Pieces
_____	_____
_____	_____
_____	_____
_____	_____
_____	_____
_____	_____

1. Which book do you think had more settings? _____

2. Why do you think the author needed to use more settings in that book?

_____

_____

_____

PRACTICE SPEAKING AND LISTENING!

Speaker 1: _____
(name)

Speaker 2: _____
(name)

Answer this question aloud and support your opinion with reasons:

Which location do you think is the most important in Counting by 7s? *Why?*

Listen to Speaker 1's answer. On a separate piece of paper, write a summary of your partner's answer.

then

Answer this question aloud and support your opinion with reasons:

Which location do you think is the most important in All the Broken Pieces? *Why?*

Listen to Speaker 2's answer. On a separate piece of paper, write a summary of your partner's answer.

Name: _____

A SENSE OF PLACE

Authors use descriptive language to make the setting come to life. Reread the passages listed below that describe a specific setting in each novel.

Fill in the chart with descriptive words and phrases from each passage that create a sense of place. What details does each author use to help you imagine this setting?

Novel	Counting by 7s	All the Broken Pieces
Setting	the Gardens of Glenwood building	the Veteran Voices meeting building
Pages	178–179 (Chapter 30) and 189 (Chapter 32)	99–101
Words and Phrases		

1. Looking back at the chart you have just completed, which descriptive word or phrase used by the author gives you the strongest sense of each place?

   the Gardens of Glenwood building: _____

   the Veteran Voices meeting building: _____

2. In your opinion, which setting was easiest to picture?

   _____

3. What made that setting easier to picture than the other one? Consider everything from the author's description of the setting to your own familiarity with similar settings.

   _____

   _____

   _____

Name(s): _____

SETTING AND MEANING

With a partner or in a small group, share your answers from the "A Sense of Place" worksheet. Then, discuss the importance of these settings and work together to answer the questions below.

1. What is the importance of each setting to the story?

   A. How is the Gardens of Glenwood building important to the story of *Counting by 7s*?

   _____

   _____

   _____

   B. How is the Veteran Voices meeting building important to *All the Broken Pieces*?

   _____

   _____

   _____

2. Next, think about how these two settings compare and contrast.

   A. What are the similarities between these settings? _____

   _____

   _____

   B. What are the differences between these settings? _____

   _____

   _____

3. Discuss the *tone* of these descriptions. What feeling about these settings do you think the authors were trying to convey with these descriptions?

   A. the Gardens of Glenwood building: _____

   _____

   B. the Veteran Voices meeting building: _____

   _____

4. Does this feeling about the setting change by the end of the novel? If so, how?

   A. the Gardens of Glenwood building: _____

   _____

   B. the Veteran Voices meeting building: _____

   _____

UNIT 4 TEACHER INSTRUCTIONS

The *theme* is the main idea or message behind the story. Students should be guided to think about the significance of each novel and how characters, setting, and plot contribute to overall meaning. Consider what these books reveal about survival, immigration, friendship, courage, perseverance, and family. In this unit, students will compare and contrast how these realistic novels treat similar themes. Students will conduct close readings of several passages in both novels to analyze and compare the way authors reveal themes through plot points and characters. Students will work together and individually to think deeply about major and minor themes that these novels share.

Introduce students to the concept of theme by distributing the top portion of "A Quick Guide to Theme" (page 35). The bottom portion offers suggestions for using Interactive Notebooks to reinforce learning. Distribute any or all of these when appropriate.

Unit 4 includes the following components. See page 5 of this book for an explanation of icons.

"Theme Seeds" (pages 36–37) — Work in small groups to compare how a theme appears in both novels and provide textual evidence.

Options:

- ▶ Assign each theme listed on the handout to a group and have each group present its work to the class.

- ▶ Before group work, have a whole-class discussion to identify the themes in the first section of the handout and then assign groups to each theme.

"Lending Their Support" (pages 38–39) — Consider the influence we can have on other people's lives. Read two passages and draw conclusions from the texts, using evidence to support answers. Culminate this activity by discussing the similarities and differences in how the novels approach theme.

"Feeling Broken" (page 40) — Explore the way title relates to theme. Perform close readings of two passages to identify how both books explore the concept of being emotionally broken and how the characters are affected by loss.

"Taking the Analysis Further" (page 41) — Build on the group work done in the previous activity. Go deeper into an analysis of the way this theme appears in both novels. Demonstrate understanding by drawing conclusions about the authors' purpose.

"Becoming Part of a Team" (pages 42–43) — Examine the concept of teamwork and use textual evidence to show how this theme is developed in each novel. Culminate this activity with a short writing assignment to synthesize ideas from both novels. (*TIP:* Before assigning this activity, have the class brainstorm characteristics of a successful team.)

"Family Matters" (page 44) — Read a passage from each novel and draw conclusions about the common theme. Find additional textual evidence and synthesize their idea in a final question.

See page 34 for the description of the essay-writing activity that culminates this unit.

UNIT 4 TEACHER INSTRUCTIONS (cont.)

Unit 4 culminates with students writing an essay that compares how the same theme is presented in the two novels. See the information in the box below for more details.

Unit 4 includes the following components. See page 5 of this book for an explanation of icons.

"Comparing a Theme" (pages 45–49) — Use a traditional format to write an informative essay about the way each book addresses a common theme.

(*TIP:* The following components will help guide students through the planning, drafting, and rewriting process. Drafts and final essays are written on separate paper.)

 "Prewriting Worksheet" (page 45) — Choose one major theme that connects the two novels. Brainstorm how each novel reveals this theme, and then make comparisons between the two novels.

 "Outline Worksheet" (page 46) — Use an outline format to organize essays. Find relevant quotations to support points about the chosen theme.

 "Self-Editing Checklist (Rough Draft)" (page 47) — Use this assignment-specific checklist to stay on task and organized after the completion of the first draft.

(*TIP:* Also use this checklist to help students complete the "Comparing Form Essay Assignment" on pages 60–61.)

 "Peer-Editing Checklist" (page 48) — Use this checklist to evaluate the essays of other students and to receive feedback prior to completing a final draft.

(*TIP:* Also use this checklist to help students complete the "Comparing Form Essay Assignment" on pages 60–61.)

 "Self-Editing Checklist (Final Draft)" (page 49) — This checklist should be used to fine-tune essays and to implement the suggestions given by peers.

(*TIP:* Also use this checklist to help students complete the "Comparing Form Essay Assignment" on pages 60–61.)

A QUICK GUIDE TO THEME

The *theme* is the main idea of the novel. It is the *message* behind what happens in the story. The *major theme* or themes are the big ideas that are present throughout the whole book. When thinking about a book's themes, consider *why* the story is important. What does it teach us or show us about life?

To help you identify themes, think about this question: *What are the big ideas that hold the story together?* For instance, one big idea might be "Friendship." The theme of the novel is what the book shows readers about friendship. What point do you think the author is trying to make about friendship? The theme could be "Friends can become like a family" or "True friends accept you for who you are."

A novel may have more than one theme. There may also be *minor themes*, which are ideas that are not in the novel as frequently or as prominently as the major themes.

> ## Unit Vocabulary
> ✓ theme
> ✓ message
> ✓ major theme
> ✓ minor theme

INTERACTIVE LITERATURE NOTEBOOK SUGGESTIONS FOR UNIT 4

1 One Word	2 Part of a Team	3 Family Member	4 The Seven	5 Interview
Think about how you would complete this sentence using only one word: *This book makes me think about* ____. Write this word in the middle of the page. Fill the rest of the page with pictures, words, and/or quotations that relate to this word. Be creative and artistic with your design.	What does it mean to be a team? Write your definition in your notebook. Use pictures of different types of teams to decorate the page. If you have been on a team, include a few sentences about how the members of that team treated each other.	Pick one of your family members whom you admire. Write a description of the person and why you admire him or her. How has this person influenced you? Include a photograph.	At the end of *Counting by 7s*, Willow lists the seven most important people in her life. Make your own list of the seven most important people in your own life and how they have influenced you.	Interview someone who has moved to the U.S. from another country to find out about his or her experience. Create a page for your questions and the person's answers.

THEME SEEDS

Counting by 7s and *All the Broken Pieces* have similar themes and ideas. A **theme** is the message behind the whole story. A novel could have several themes. For instance, here are some ideas that apply to both of these novels. Your group will select one of these topics and analyze how both books develop this theme.

What do the novels show readers about these topics?

❑ Family   ❑ Starting Over   ❑ Being Different

❑ Friendship   ❑ Loss and Grief   ❑ Having Compassion

❑ Perseverance

Choose one of the above topics to analyze. Put a checkmark in the box beside your choice, and then answer the questions below and on the following page.

Counting by 7s

What happens in this novel that shows this theme? _____

_____

_____

_____

Provide one quotation that supports your answer. (from page number: _____)

_____

_____

All the Broken Pieces

What happens in this novel that shows this theme? _____

_____

_____

_____

Provide one quotation that supports your answer. (from page number: _____)

_____

_____

Name(s): _____

THEME SEEDS (cont.)

In the box below, write the theme you chose on the previous page. Then answer the following questions in order to compare and contrast the two novels.

Compare

1. How are these novels similar in the way they present this theme?

_____

_____

_____

_____

2. Why do you think both authors chose this same way to approach this particular theme?

_____

_____

_____

_____

Contrast

1. How are these novels different in the way they present this theme?

_____

_____

_____

_____

2. Why do you think each author chose to approach this theme differently? Why are the different approaches necessary for each novel?

_____

_____

_____

_____

Name: _____

LENDING THEIR SUPPORT

Counting by 7s and *All the Broken Pieces* show the positive impact we can have when we help and support each other. This theme is demonstrated in many ways in both novels. Look closely at the scenes listed below and consider how the authors develop this theme.

from *Counting by 7s*	from *All the Broken Pieces*
pages 94–95 and 284 (about Jairo)	pages 97–111 and 155–161

1. How does Jairo feel about Willow?

   _____

   _____

2. Why do you think Jairo feels this way?

   _____

   _____

3. What does Willow think of Jairo's opinion of her?

   _____

   _____

4. Why do you think Willow feels this way?

   _____

   _____

5. Who do you agree with, Willow or Jairo?

   _____

   Explain your reasons and give at least two examples or quotations from the book to support your opinion.

   _____

   _____

   _____

   _____

   _____

   _____

   _____

LENDING THEIR SUPPORT (cont.)

6. In *All the Broken Pieces*, Jeff and Matt's parents think that having Matt at the Veteran Voices meeting will help the veterans. Why might Matt's presence at the meeting help the veterans?

_____

_____

7. After the first meeting, does Matt feel that he helped anyone? Explain your answer.

_____

_____

8. In the end, how did having Matt at these meetings help the veterans? What did it help them realize and remember? Give at least two examples or quotations to support your answer.

_____

_____

_____

_____

COMPARING THE NOVELS

9. How are Matt and Willow similar in the ways they think of themselves?

_____

_____

_____

10. How are they similar in the ways they influence other people?

_____

_____

_____

11. What do you think the authors of these novels want readers to realize about our interactions with other people?

_____

_____

_____

Name(s): _____

FEELING BROKEN

An author chooses a title that reflects the meaning of the book. A title may even have several meanings. Think about the title *All the Broken Pieces* and the different meanings this title could have. How does this title capture the theme of the novel? Could this title also apply to *Counting by 7s*? Work together to analyze the passages listed below.

Read the poem on pages 22–23 of *All the Broken Pieces*. (It begins, "I close my eyes.")

1. What is the poem about? _____

   _____

   _____

2. What does Matt mean by "broken pieces" in this poem?

   _____

   _____

Now read Chapter 22 in *Counting by 7s* (pages 131–138).

3. How is Willow's experience and reaction similar to Matt's? Give examples and at least one quotation.

   _____

   _____

   _____

   _____

4. By the end of the novels, are these characters still "broken"? Explain and give an example for each character.

   Matt: _____

   _____

   _____

   Willow: _____

   _____

   _____

5. Would "All the Broken Pieces" work as a title for *Counting by 7s*? Explain.

   _____

   _____

   _____

Name: _____

TAKING THE ANALYSIS FURTHER

In the previous activity, you worked with a group to analyze how Matt and Willow are "broken." Think about the ways this idea of being "broken" applies to other characters. Using evidence from both novels, identify how this theme is developed with other characters.

Identify from each novel two secondary characters who are "broken."

		Character	Why?	Quotation and Page Number
All the Broken Pieces	1.			
	2.			
Counting by 7s	1.			
	2.			

Are these characters still broken (or *as* broken) by the end of the novels? Explain.

_____

_____

_____

PUT IT ALL TOGETHER

This theme of being emotionally broken is developed throughout both novels. On a separate sheet of paper, write a paragraph that explains what point you think these authors are making by presenting these broken characters. What do they want readers to realize? End your paragraph by explaining how you came to this conclusion?

UNIT 4: THEME

BECOMING PART OF A TEAM

In *All the Broken Pieces*, Matt's dad encourages him to try out for baseball and tells him that it is good to be part of a team. Consider whether or not this was true for Matt and Willow.

1. Think about Matt's experience on the baseball team. Explain why he did not always feel as though he was part of the team.

_____

_____

_____

Find and record a quotation that supports your answer: _____

_____

_____

_____

Page number: _____

2. What were some of the positive experiences Matt had as a part of the team?

_____

_____

_____

Find and record a quotation that supports your answer: _____

_____

_____

_____

Page number: _____

3. Even though Matt went though some difficult experiences on the baseball team, how did being part of the team help him grow and change?

_____

_____

_____

_____

_____

_____

Name: _____

BECOMING PART OF A TEAM (cont.)

In *Counting by 7s*, Willow becomes a part of a different type of team.

4. Explain how the Nguyens, Dell Duke, Jairo, and Willow were a team.

_____

_____

_____

_____

Find and record a quotation that supports your answer: _____

_____

_____

Page number: _____

5. Willow's team was not perfect, although she did not encounter the same struggles that Matt did. Give one example that shows a character on Willow's team not being a good team member.

_____

_____

_____

Find and record a quotation that supports your answer: _____

_____

_____

Page number: _____

6. How did becoming part of this team help Willow grow and change?

_____

_____

_____

PUT IT ALL TOGETHER

On a separate sheet of paper, write a paragraph in which you explain who you think was helped the most by their team, Willow or Matt. Also explain what you think both authors were trying to show readers about working as a team.

Name: _____

FAMILY MATTERS

One important theme that is explored in *Counting by 7s* and *All the Broken Pieces* is adoption.

1. Read Willow's physical description of her family in Chapter 2 (pages 11–12) of *Counting by 7s*. Explain what you think Willow means when she says they look like a family even though they do not look alike.

   _____

   _____

   _____

   _____

2. Find textual evidence from another part of the novel that shows Willow's relationship with her parents. Include the page number at the end of the quotation.

   _____

   _____

   _____

3. Now read Matt's conversation with his adoptive parents on page 205 of *All the Broken Pieces*. Explain why this conversation is important.

   _____

   _____

   _____

4. Find textual evidence from another part of the novel that shows Matt's relationship with his adoptive parents. Include the page number at the end of the quotation.

   _____

   _____

   _____

5. Explain how Matt's and Willow's adoptive families are similar and what message the authors of these novels might want readers to understand about adoptive families.

   _____

   _____

   _____

   _____

   _____

Name: _____

COMPARING A THEME

PREWRITING WORKSHEET

Write an essay that compares the way each book addresses a specific theme. To compare two novels in a subject-by-subject essay, first start with your claim about the theme in both books. Then, in the body paragraphs, discuss one book at a time. Use these guidelines to help you plan your essay.

Counting by 7s and *All the Broken Pieces* share several important themes about traumatic events, family, perseverance, fitting in, and adapting to change. Which of these themes do you think is the most important theme in both novels?

Most Important Theme: _____

Explain why you think this is the most important theme. _____

_____

_____

_____

Do some brainstorming to generate ideas. How is this theme shown in each novel?

Counting by 7s	*All the Broken Pieces*
_____	_____
_____	_____
_____	_____

1. Are the books more similar or different in the ways they show this theme? Explain why.

_____

_____

_____

2. Do you think one book did a better job of showing this theme? Explain your answer.

_____

_____

_____

Name: _____

COMPARING A THEME (cont.)

OUTLINE WORKSHEET

Use your brainstorming notes to help you plan your essay. Write key words and phrases in each section of the outline. Then use the outline as a guide when you draft your essay.

I. Introduction Paragraph: Your Thesis Statement

- Make a claim about how the novels are similar or different in the ways they show this theme.

  _____

  _____

II. Example from *Counting by 7s*

- Explain how *Counting by 7s* shows this theme.

  _____

  _____

- Give at least one quotation as evidence.

- Explain why this quotation is important.

III. Example from *All the Broken Pieces*

- Explain how *All the Broken Pieces* shows this theme.

  _____

  _____

- Give at least one quotation as evidence.

- Explain why this quotation is important.

IV. Conclusion Paragraph

- Explain why this theme is important for readers to understand.

- Discuss whether the books are more similar or different in the ways they show this theme.

> *TIP:* When you write your essay, be sure to use phrases that show comparison and contrast. Here are some examples:
>
> | | | |
> |---|---|---|
> | Similar to | Like | Compared to |
> | However | Unlike | In contrast |

Name: _____

COMPARING A THEME (cont.)

SELF-EDITING CHECKLIST (ROUGH DRAFT)

Use this checklist to make sure your rough draft has everything that is required. Check off the box next to each item once you have included that element in your essay.

- ❏ My introduction states the topic of my essay and the point I will make about it.

- ❏ I have used quotations from *Counting by 7s*. How many? _____

- ❏ I have used quotations from *All the Broken Pieces*. How many? _____

- ❏ I have included page numbers of quotations from the novels.

- ❏ I have explained all quotations.

- ❏ I have used transition words that show comparison and contrast.

- ❏ My conclusion states the importance of my topic.

- ❏ My conclusion explains how the books are similar or different.

- ❏ I read over my essay to check for spelling, punctuation, and grammar mistakes.

One thing I like about my essay is _____

_____

_____

_____

One thing I am not sure about is _____

_____

_____

_____

_____

One thing I need help with is _____

_____

_____

_____

_____

COMPARING A THEME (cont.)

PEER-EDITING CHECKLIST

Reader's Name: _____ Writer's Name: _____

Read your partner's essay and check a box for each statement.

	Yes	No
The introduction does a good job explaining the point the writer will make.	❏	❏
There are quotations from *Counting by 7s* in this essay.	❏	❏
How many? _____		
There are quotations from *All the Broken Pieces* in this essay.	❏	❏
How many? _____		
The essay uses the right comparison words and phrases to help show the relationship between ideas. (Are there any places that need more of these types of phrases? If so, mark them on the paper.)	❏	❏
The conclusion explains why the topic is important.	❏	❏
The conclusion makes sense and fits with the rest of the essay.	❏	❏
There are no spelling errors or sentence mistakes.	❏	❏

Look closely at how well the writer explained each point. The paragraph that does this best is #_____.

Why? _____

_____

A paragraph that is confusing or unclear is #_____. What questions did you have about this paragraph?

_____

_____

What did you like best about this essay? _____

_____

_____

What is one more thing the writer can do to make the essay better? _____

_____

_____

Name: _____

COMPARING A THEME (cont.)

SELF-EDITING CHECKLIST (FINAL DRAFT)

After your peer editor or editors read your essay and give you comments, use those comments and suggestions to revise your essay.

TIP: After you revise your essay, try reading it out loud one more time. Sometimes it is easier to find mistakes when you read your essay out loud to yourself.

Answer these questions after your final draft is complete.

(Circle one.) My first draft had   **no   some   many**   spelling and grammar mistakes.

I am still not sure about _____

_____

_____

_____

_____

_____

After reading the comments on my paper, I added _____

_____

_____

_____

_____

_____

The most important change I made on my draft was _____

_____

_____

_____

_____

_____

UNIT 5 TEACHER INSTRUCTIONS

Examining writer's *craft* requires students to consider the author's intentions and how writing choices suit the purpose or artistry of a story. Many of the activities in the previous units and the single-novel units (pages 62–92) address writer's craft in the context of literary elements. This section offers additional activities to further develop your students' understanding of author's craft.

In this unit, students will examine each novel's overall structure, paying attention to both authors' use of dividing the novels into sections and chapters. Students will also analyze word choice as it relates to tone, consider the effectiveness of point of view, and compare poetry to prose.

Introduce students to the concepts of craft and structure by distributing "A Quick Guide to Craft and Structure" (pages 51–52). The bottom portion of page 52 offers suggestions for using Interactive Notebooks to reinforce learning. Distribute any or all of these when appropriate.

Unit 5 includes the following components. See page 5 of this book for an explanation of icons.

 "Identifying Tone" (page 53) — Examine how words and phrases can contribute to the tone of a story or scene. Apply understanding by selecting a passage to analyze and identifying language that determines the tone of the chosen passage.

 "Symbolism: A Peek Inside" (page 54) — Read a passage in *All the Broken Pieces* and discuss the author's use of symbolism. Apply the meaning of symbol to themes and characters in both books.

 "Symbolism: Building Connections" (page 55) — Build on an understanding of symbolism by analyzing symbolism in a passage from *Counting by 7s* and applying the idea to both novels.

 "Form Flip" (pages 56–57) — Consider poetry and prose forms, what each style contributes to the overall work, and how the novels would change if written in a different form. Perform a close reading of two passages and identify quotes that demonstrate strong poetic and prosaic writing. Rewrite these same passages as prose and poetry, and assess how effective the novels would be in the other form. (*TIP:* Have students share their answers on the first page of the worksheet before moving on to the second page. Discuss the qualities of poetry versus prose.)

 "Considering Point of View" (pages 58–59) — Use this activity to think critically about the way point of view impacts story. Consider how a change in narration from first-person to third-person would affect each novel.

 "Comparing Form Essay Assignment" (pages 60–61) — Write an informative essay that compares the forms of the two novels. Complete a pre-writing worksheet in order to generate ideas and find a focus. (*TIP:* This activity also provides a model format to help students plan and draft their essays.)

A QUICK GUIDE TO CRAFT AND STRUCTURE

When writing a book, an author must make many choices. These choices affect the meaning and style of the book, and they greatly influence the reader's experience.

Forms of Writing

Literature comes in a variety of forms, such as prose, poetry, or drama. A novel written in *prose* uses sentences and paragraphs to express ideas. Prose writing sounds similar to the way we speak. *Poetry* uses creative line breaks, stanzas, and vivid language to express feelings, emotions, and images in fewer words than prose. Free-verse poetry is a type of poetry that does not use a specific pattern of rhyme or meter. There are many novels that have been written in free-verse poetry rather than prose.

Organization and Structure

The author can use various methods of organizing the text, from small units such as **paragraphs** or **stanzas**, to larger units such as **chapters**, **sections**, or **parts**. The author has a purpose in dividing the novel into these structures. As you read, think about how the author organizes the story and how the *structure* helps your understanding of the novel.

Point of View

The *point of view* is the *voice* in which the novel is written. The author's choice of a specific point of view for a novel relates to his or her purpose. The author may want readers to feel a deeper connection with one character and hear the story from just his or her perspective. Or the author may want the reader to have a more thorough understanding of all the characters and events in the story.

✳ *First-Person:* The narrator is a character in the story who describes what he or she sees, hears, feels, and thinks. The character uses words like "I" and "we." A first-person narrator can only tell the reader as much as his or her character knows.

✳ *Third-Person:* The narrator is not a character in the story. This type of narration does not use words like "I" and "we." Third-person can be omniscient or limited. An *omniscient* narrator can describe any events and all of the characters' thoughts and actions, even when the main character is not present. A *limited* third-person point of view still uses "he" and "she" but describes situations in which the main character is involved.

Tone and Mood

The author uses word choice, setting, and details to create the *tone* and *mood* of a story or scene. The author's tone shows the reader how the author feels about the subject. When a story is written in first-person, the tone can show how the narrator feels about the subject. For example, an angry tone may be used for a scene about someone being treated unfairly.

The author's tone helps create the mood of the scene. Mood is the way the writing makes the reader feel. Authors pick descriptive words and use figurative language to give readers a feeling about the scene.

Unit Vocabulary
- ✓ prose
- ✓ poetry
- ✓ structure
- ✓ point of view
- ✓ voice
- ✓ omniscient
- ✓ limited
- ✓ tone
- ✓ mood
- ✓ meaning
- ✓ literal (explicit)
- ✓ implied (inferred)
- ✓ inference
- ✓ symbolism

A QUICK GUIDE TO CRAFT AND STRUCTURE (cont.)

Inference

Text can have both a *literal* meaning and an *implied* meaning. *Literal* or *explicit* meaning is what the passage actually says. The words directly state information. *Implied* or *inferred* meaning is information that is not stated in the text but can be determined due to our previous knowledge and to clues provided in the text.

Example: Johnny rushed into class 10 minutes after the bell rang. His hair stuck out in all directions, his coat was mis-buttoned, and he was wearing slippers. Mrs. Maddox rolled her eyes and said, "Again, Johnny? Maybe it's time to get a new alarm clock."

* **Literal meaning:** Johnny is late to class. Johnny looks messy and is wearing slippers instead of shoes. This information is all directly explained in the text.

* **Implied meaning:** Johnny overslept, and this has happened before. The passage does not directly state that Johnny overslept, but there are clues that help the reader make that assumption. This logical conclusion is called an *inference*.

Symbolism

Symbolism is when an author uses one thing to represent something else. The symbol has a deeper meaning that may be related to theme or character. Authors may refer to the same symbol many times throughout the novel, or they may use a symbol one time to emphasize a significant point.

INTERACTIVE LITERATURE NOTEBOOK SUGGESTIONS FOR UNIT 5

1 You'll Love It!	2 This Sentence Says It All	3 How It Made Me Feel	4 Found Poem	5 My Poem
Do you know somebody who would love the style of this book? Write a note to the person explaining why you think he or she will enjoy this book.	As you read, look for sentences that stand out and are meaningful to you. Create a page of your favorite quotations from the book.	How did this book make you feel as you read it? Create a page of words, pictures, and colors that describes the tone of the book.	Imagine that one of the characters in *All the Broken Pieces* finds one of the poems Matt has written. Write a paragraph from that character's point of view. Have the character react to the poem.	Write a poem that captures your observations and feelings about something that happened to you.

Name(s): _____

IDENTIFYING TONE

The author chooses words and sentence structure to create the *tone* of the book or scene. The tone may change several times in the novel, depending on what is happening in the scenes. You and your partner will read a passage in each novel and discuss the tone in that scene. Work together to identify how each author selects words and phrases to create a feeling about the author or character's attitude. Begin by analyzing the following passages:

	Counting by 7s (Chapter 29, page 175)	*All the Broken Pieces* (pages 58–60)
What is the tone of this passage?		
Identify the words and phrases that help you determine the tone.		

1. How are these two scenes similar? _____

   _____

   _____

2. Why do you think the authors use this type of tone at this point in the story?

   _____

Find an example from one of the novels of a completely different tone.

   Novel: _____   Page number(s): _____

3. What is happening in this passage? _____

   _____

   _____

4. What is the tone? _____

   _____

5. Identify words and phrases that help you determine the tone. _____

   _____

   _____

Name(s): _____

SYMBOLISM: A PEEK INSIDE

Read the poems on pages 121–123 of *All the Broken Pieces*. Coach Robeson has his team take apart baseballs to look inside. Read the entire passage carefully and notice the way the entire process is described. With a partner or small group, discuss what the baseball in this passage symbolizes and how this symbol relates to the themes and characters of this novel as well as those in *Counting by 7s*.

1. In this passage, what is the baseball a symbol for? Discuss why the coach has the kids take apart the baseballs and what he wants them to learn.

    _____

    _____

    _____

    _____

2. When the kids get to the rubber ball at the center of the baseball, the coach asks the team how many of them think they have reached the core. They all say yes but soon find out they are wrong. What is the deeper meaning of this passage, beyond what is at the center of a baseball?

    _____

    _____

    _____

    _____

    _____

3. How does this symbol relate to the themes and characters in *All the Broken Pieces*?

    _____

    _____

    _____

    _____

4. Now discuss how this symbol might apply to *Counting by 7s*. Use examples from *Counting by 7s* to support your explanation.

    _____

    _____

    _____

    _____

    _____

SYMBOLISM: BUILDING CONNECTIONS

In *Counting by 7s*, the Gardens of Glenwood apartment building serves as an important symbol. Read page 307 (in Chapter 49) about the changes to the outside of the building. In this passage, Willow describes what is happening to the building and says it shows connectedness. She talks only about the building, but the reader should be able to infer a deeper meaning to her words.

1. In your own words, explain what Willow means by "connectedness." What is the deeper meaning beyond the description of the building?

_____

_____

_____

_____

2. How does this image of the building's connectedness symbolize what is happening to the characters in the story? Compare what Willow says about the building to the things that happen between the characters.

_____

_____

_____

_____

PUT IT ALL TOGETHER

Now think about how this idea of "connectedness" applies to Matt and the other characters in *All the Broken Pieces*. Compare Willow's building description to the idea of "connectedness" in *All the Broken Pieces*. Use examples from *All the Broken Pieces* to support your explanation.

_____

_____

_____

_____

_____

_____

_____

_____

FORM FLIP

All the Broken Pieces tells Matt's story through a series of poems. Reread the poem on page 65, in which Matt considers running away. Select a few lines from this poem that you think are particularly powerful or vivid. Quote them here:

```
[                                                          ]
```

1. What makes these lines good examples of poetic form?

_____

_____

_____

_____

2. Think about the way poetry affects the reader and conveys Matt's feelings. Why do you think the author chose to write Matt's story in poetry rather than prose?

_____

_____

_____

_____

Counting by 7s is told in prose. Review Chapter 26. Find a short passage (2–3 sentences) that you think shows good use of prose. Quote it here:

```
[                                                          ]
```

3. What makes these sentences a good example of prose form?

_____

_____

_____

_____

Name: _____

FORM FLIP (cont.)

Do you think the reader's experience would be very different if these novels were written in different forms? To get a better understanding of the way form affects story, first try to rewrite a short passage from each book in a different form.

Novel: _Counting by 7s_   **Scene:** chapter 26, where Willow runs away to the library

Rewrite this scene as a poem. Try using key words and phrases from the passage to help you get started.

_____

_____

_____

_____

_____

_____

Novel: _All the Broken Pieces_   **Scene:** page 65, where Matt considers running away

Rewrite this part of the novel as if Matt were describing his thoughts in a paragraph, not poetry. Think about how he would explain his reasons and what other details he would include about his mother.

_____

_____

_____

_____

_____

Do you think these books would work as well if they switched forms? For each, circle **Yes** or **No**. Then explain your answers.

Counting by 7s   **Yes**   **No**   Why or why not? _____

_____

All the Broken Pieces   **Yes**   **No**   Why or why not? _____

_____

CONSIDERING POINT OF VIEW

Counting by 7s and *All the Broken Pieces* are both written in first-person point of view; however, *Counting by 7s* also has chapters told in third-person. This allows the readers to find out information that Willow would not know. Point of view changes the way a story is told. It also affects how much the reader knows about all the characters. Work with a partner or small group to discuss how these books would change if they were told from a different point of view.

1. *All the Broken Pieces* is written in first-person, from Matt's perspective. What if this novel had included some chapters written in third-person, like *Counting by 7s* does? What other details do you think could have been added to the novel that Matt would not have known?

   _____

   _____

   _____

2. Do you think you would have the same understanding of what Matt was going through if the entire novel had been written in third-person? Explain your answer.

   _____

   _____

   _____

   _____

Reread the poem on page 63 in *All the Broken Pieces*. Since Matt is telling the story, we are limited to his interpretation of what his parents are talking about.

3. If *All the Broken Pieces* had been written in third-person, what other details do you think the reader would have found out about the parents' argument?

   _____

   _____

   _____

   _____

4. Do you think changing the story to third-person would make the story better or worse? Explain your answer.

   _____

   _____

   _____

   _____

CONSIDERING POINT OF VIEW (cont.)

5. If *Counting by 7s* had been written from only Willow's point of view instead of including chapters in third-person, what information would the reader not get?

_____

_____

_____

6. What do the third-person chapters add to the story?

_____

_____

_____

_____

Read Chapter 56. Think about what all of the characters think, do, and say in this chapter.

7. What do we learn in this chapter that is different from Willow's perspective?

_____

_____

_____

PUT IT ALL TOGETHER

8. Why do you think these authors chose to use first-person to tell Matt and Willow's stories?

_____

_____

_____

_____

9. Which novel do you think would be easier to write entirely in third-person?

_____

Why? _____

_____

_____

Name: _____

COMPARING FORM ESSAY ASSIGNMENT

Prewriting Worksheet

You will use the following pages to plan and write a point-by-point comparison essay. In order to write this type of essay, you start with a claim about both novels. Each body paragraph of your essay focuses on one similarity or difference between the novels and uses examples from both novels.

Begin by brainstorming ideas. How are the books similar even though one is prose and one is poetry? List as many ideas as you can think of.

_____

_____

_____

How is reading a story told through poetry different from reading one told in prose?

Here are some ideas to help you get started:

- Did one form help you understand the character's feelings better?

- Did one form make the story feel more complete?

- Did poetry make the book easier or more difficult to read than prose?

_____

_____

_____

_____

Thesis Statement Starter

Look through your notes above and decide what similarities and differences you want to write about. What do you want to tell readers about the differences in reading a book in prose versus a book in poetry? Use your thoughts to construct a thesis statement, from which your entire essay will follow. The following sample will help you to do this:

Although *Counting by 7s* is written in prose and *All the Broken Pieces* is written in verse, they both

_____

_____

However, telling the story through poetry _____

_____

_____

60

Name: _____

COMPARING FORM ESSAY ASSIGNMENT *(cont.)*

Create an outline for your essay. Write down key words and ideas here:

I. Introduction

Introduce your essay. Provide the thesis, from which the entire essay will follow.

_____

_____

_____

_____

II. First Point

Pick one similarity or difference. Name it here: _____

_____

   A. Provide an example from *Counting by 7s.*

   B. Provide an example from *All the Broken Pieces.*

   C. Explain how the two novels are similar or different.

III. A Second Point

Pick another similarity or difference. Name it here: _____

_____

   A. Provide an example from *Counting by 7s.*

   B. Provide an example from *All the Broken Pieces.*

   C. Explain how the two novels are similar or different.

IV. A Third Point

Pick another similarity or difference. Name it here: _____

_____

   A. Provide an example from *Counting by 7s.*

   B. Provide an example from *All the Broken Pieces.*

   C. Explain how the two novels are similar or different.

V. Conclusion

Wrap up your essay. Connect all the points together and summarize your thoughts.

INTRODUCTION TO SECTION II

The worksheets in the first section of this book encourage your students to make connections between the novels and think deeply about the way these novels approach similar topics and themes. The main goal of this book is to provide a wide range of activities that require students to compare the ideas, craft, and structure of these works.

Before your students can complete the activities that make up the focus of this book, they must first read and study each novel separately. To that end, the contents in this section are intended to provide you with single-novel activities that relate to concepts your students will encounter in the comparison activities. This section is not a comprehensive packet of single-novel worksheets, but rather it is a brief supplement that can be used in conjunction with the Interactive Notebook activities, your own single-novel activities, or other single-novel study guides.

In addition to the worksheets in this section, the Interactive Literature Notebook suggestions at the beginning of Units 1–5 will provide your students with creative ways to reinforce their understanding of literary elements in general and comprehension of these novels specifically. These Interactive Literature Notebook ideas provide you with a wide range of options for reinforcing your teaching of story elements and structure as you and your students read each novel.

The single-novel activities are divided into three units:

Unit 6 — pages 63–68

This unit includes individual activities that can be used with either novel. To get started, see the Teacher Instructions on page 63.

Unit 7 — pages 69–81

This unit includes activities specifically tailored to be used with *Counting by 7s*. To get started, see the Teacher Instructions on page 69.

Unit 8 — pages 82–93

This unit includes activities specifically tailored to be used with *All the Broken Pieces*. To get started, see the Teacher Instructions on page 82.

UNIT 6 TEACHER INSTRUCTIONS

The worksheets in this section provide general practice activities for use with either or both novels. All activities in this section are individual activities, although several can be adapted easily for collaborative or whole-class discussion.

Unit 6 includes the following components. See page 5 of this book for an explanation of icons.

"My Word Wall" (page 64) — Identify unknown words while reading the novel. Practice using context clues as well as reference materials to understand word meaning.

(*TIP:* You may want to have each student suggest a word from his or her worksheet to create a Class Word Wall for further study and testing.)

"An Important Event" (page 65) — Build summarization skills and increase understanding of story elements. Examine how a specific scene relates to the overall structure of the story.

"What If?" (page 66) — This activity is a follow-up exercise based on the worksheet "An Important Event." Use it to further develop an understanding of how a scene or chapter affects the overall story.

"Writing a Persuasive Letter" (page 67) — Use a letter-writing format to construct an argument and support that opinion with evidence from the text.

(*TIP:* Have students share their letters with each other for proofreading and editing practice.)

"My Book Rating" (page 68) — Use a rating system to evaluate different components of the story before making a final evaluation of the book as a whole.

MY WORD WALL

Find your own vocabulary words. As you read the novel, look for words you don't know. Use this chart to write down the words and their meanings.

My Own Sentence	Dictionary Definition	My Guess	Sentence and Page Number	Word

AN IMPORTANT EVENT

The plot is the series of events that make up the story. The author carefully creates events that show how the conflict, or main problem, of the story builds and resolves. Each point in the plot is important to the overall structure of the story. Think about how the events in the book fit together to tell the whole story.

Select one important event in the novel to analyze.

What are the page numbers of this scene? _____

Which characters were involved? _____

_____

Summarize what happens in this scene. _____

_____

_____

_____

_____

What caused the event in this scene? Why did it happen? _____

_____

_____

_____

Find one quotation that is important to the scene. _____

_____

_____

Page number: _____

Why is this an important scene? How does it fit into the whole story?

_____

_____

_____

_____

_____

_____

_____

WHAT IF?

In the last activity, you picked one event that is part of the plot and explained why it was important to the overall story. Further explore this event and its impact on the overall novel.

How does that scene end? _____

_____

_____

_____

Why do you think it ends that way? _____

_____

_____

_____

Think of another way this scene could have ended. Describe the new ending here.

_____

_____

_____

_____

If the scene ended that way, how would the rest of the story change?

_____

_____

_____

_____

Would this change make the story better or worse? Explain why.

_____

_____

_____

_____

WRITING A PERSUASIVE LETTER

Imagine a school in another town is considering using this novel in their 7th- and 8th-grade classes. They want to hear from students who have read the book and find out what they think. Write a letter to the school board explaining why you would or would not recommend this novel for their school. What do you like or not like about the writing? How do you think other kids will relate to the book?

Follow this outline and write your letter on a separate piece of paper.

Paragraph 1 should include this information:

- State whether or not you recommend the book.
- Explain your experience with the book. (When did you read it? Why did you read it? What did you think as you read it?)

Paragraph 2 should include this information:

- Explain one thing you thought was good or bad about this book. You can talk about style, characters, plot, theme, point of view, or any other writing-related topic.
- Give one example from the book that demonstrates your point.

Paragraph 3 should include this information:

- Explain another thing you liked or did not like about this book. Select from the same writing-related topics listed in the Paragraph 2 instructions.
- Give one example from the book that demonstrates your point.

Paragraph 4 should include this information:

- Explain how you think the students will respond to this book. Focus on the way it will make them feel or think about the situation described in the novel.
- Give one example from the book and explain how you felt when you read it.

Paragraph 5 should include this information:

- Write a conclusion that restates your recommendation and explains why it is important.

Dear School Board,

Paragraph 1 goes here.

Paragraph 2 goes here.

Paragraph 3 goes here.

Paragraph 4 goes here.

Paragraph 5 goes here.

Sincerely,

sign name ➞ *Your signature*

print name ➞ **Your name**

MY BOOK RATING

What did you like or dislike about this book? Think about the story elements and rank each one between 0 and 5 stars. Use the following rating scale:

0 stars	1 star	2 stars	3 stars	4 stars	5 stars
☆☆☆☆☆	★☆☆☆☆	★★☆☆☆	★★★☆☆	★★★★☆	★★★★★
terrible	bad	okay	good	great	amazing!

Characters ☆☆☆☆☆

Reason: _____

Setting ☆☆☆☆☆

Reason: _____

Point of View ☆☆☆☆☆

Reason: _____

Plot ☆☆☆☆☆

Reason: _____

The Ending ☆☆☆☆☆

Reason: _____

Theme ☆☆☆☆☆

Reason: _____

Overall, I give this book _____ stars because _____

_____

_____

UNIT 7 TEACHER INSTRUCTIONS

The worksheets in this section provide activities intended specifically to be used with the novel *Counting by 7s.*

Unit 7 includes the following components. See page 5 of this book for an explanation of icons.

 "Describing Setting" (pages 70–71) — On the first page of this activity, examine how authors create setting through specific details and descriptive words. After identifying examples, explain how the setting changes. On the second page of this activity, practice speaking and listening skills by taking turns answering questions about the way setting relates to character and plot. Listeners paraphrase and respond to speakers, and then they switch roles.

 "Summary Skills" (page 72) — Read guidelines for summary writing and then write a brief summary of the novel. (*TIP:* Strong summary-writing skills are essential for college success, and students need practice in this type of writing.)

 "The Novel's Other Characters" (page 73) — Work in pairs to analyze a secondary character and create an interview. Each team will role-play their character and interviewer in front of the class. (*TIP:* Assign one of the secondary characters listed on the worksheet to each pair of students. Since there are not very many characters in the novel, you will most likely need to assign the same character to more than one group. This could allow for additional discussion of the types of questions each group created and the similarities or differences in their responses.)

 "Four Characters, One Scene" (pages 74–75) — Read deeply and consider how characterization in one passage relates to the character relationships and behaviors throughout the novel.

 "Dynamic Helpers" (pages 76–77) — Examine the ways in which three secondary characters change in response to meeting Willow. After analyzing characters and finding evidence, write a longer response defending an opinion.

 "Another Point of View" (page 78) — Use inference to develop the point of view of one of the secondary characters and to write a paragraph from that character's perspective.

 "Sharing Points of View" (page 79) — Share paragraphs from the previous page, respond to them, and work together to analyze the significance of the author's choice.

 "I Predict" (page 80) — Review the novel and make predictions based on evidence about the future of key characters in the novel.

 "Create a Novel Poster" (page 81) — Practice speaking and listening skills by collaborating in small groups to create posters that represent individual chapters in the novel. Work together to determine key points in a specific chapter, determining the chapter's relevance to the overall structure of the novel. (*TIP:* Use the "Conduct a Gallery Walk" activity from page 91 to further the experience. See the description of that activity, which is provided on page 82.)

DESCRIBING SETTING

One of the most important settings in *Counting by 7s* is Dell Duke's apartment. Examine how the author chooses words and phrases to create a vivid setting. Skim the chapters listed below to find passages that describe Dell's apartment. For each chapter, tell what Dell's apartment is like at that time and also list words and phrases that make the setting come to life.

What is Dell's apartment like in **Chapter 11**? _____

_____

Words and Phrases the Author Uses: _____

_____

What is Dell's apartment like in **Chapter 32**? _____

_____

Words and Phrases the Author Uses: _____

_____

What is Dell's apartment like in **Chapter 34**? _____

_____

Words and Phrases the Author Uses: _____

_____

What is Dell's apartment like in **Chapter 38**? _____

_____

Words and Phrases the Author Uses: _____

_____

How does Dell's apartment change over the course of the novel?

_____

_____

_____

_____

_____

Name(s): _____

DESCRIBING SETTING (cont.)

Reread Chapter 20 of *Counting by 7s*. In this chapter, the author describes the Nguyens' garage apartment. With your partner, discuss the following questions and write down your answers.

1. How would you describe the Nguyens' living situation before they moved into Dell's apartment?

_____

_____

_____

_____

2. What words and phrases did the author use to make the setting come to life?

_____

_____

_____

_____

_____

PRACTICE SPEAKING AND LISTENING!

Speaker 1: _____
(name)

Speaker 2: _____
(name)

Answer the following question aloud and support your opinion with examples from the novel: *How do the changes in Dell's apartment represent changes in the Nguyens' lives?*		Listen to Speaker 1's answer. Paraphrase your partner's answer aloud. Then say whether you agree or disagree with your partner's opinion. Explain your answer to your partner. *then* Answer the following question aloud and support your opinion with examples from the novel: *How do the changes in Dell's apartment represent changes in Dell's life?*
Listen to Speaker 2's answer. Paraphrase your partner's answer aloud. Then say whether you agree or disagree with your partner's opinion. Explain your answer to your partner.		

SUMMARY SKILLS

A *summary* is a short explanation of the main points of a longer work. To write a summary of a novel, use your own words to describe what the story is about. Do not include your opinion or reaction to the writing. Summaries simply report information. To help you build your summary skills, use the "5 Ws and H" (<u>W</u>ho, <u>W</u>hat, <u>W</u>hen, <u>W</u>here, <u>W</u>hy, and <u>H</u>ow) to help you identify the important facts.

1. Who are the important characters in the novel?

   _____

   _____

2. When does the story take place? How much time passes in the novel?

   _____

   _____

3. Where does the story take place—in what city, and in what specific places within that city?

   _____

   _____

   _____

4. What problem happens that brings the characters together?

   _____

   _____

   _____

5. Why do the characters come together because of this problem?

   _____

   _____

   _____

6. How do the characters resolve the problem?

   _____

   _____

   _____

PUTTING IT ALL TOGETHER

Use your answers to help you write a one-paragraph summary of the novel. Write your summary on the back of this handout or on a separate sheet of paper.

Name(s): _____

THE NOVEL'S OTHER CHARACTERS

Willow is the main character in *Counting by 7s*, but the other characters are important, too. The secondary characters help readers understand the main character better and help move the plot along. You and a partner will analyze one secondary character and create a mock interview that demonstrates the character's personality.

> **Your teacher will assign one of these secondary characters to you and your partner.**
>
> | Mai | Pattie | Jairo | Sadhu |
> | --- | --- | --- | --- |
> | Quang-ha | Dell Duke | Lenore Cole | Henry Pollack |
>
> **Write your assigned character's name here:** _____

You and your partner will present a live interview of your assigned character. One of you will pretend to be the character, and the other will be the interviewer. Work together to plan your interview. Write five questions you would like to ask your assigned character. Use questions that require more than a one-word answer. There are four question starters below to help you. Create your own question for #5.

1. Tell us about _____

2. What did you think when _____

3. How would you _____

4. Explain why _____

5. _____

_____

Discuss how the character would answer these questions. Then practice your presentation.

> *TIPS:*
>
> * **Interviewer:** Give the audience a brief introduction to the character, explain how the character knows Willow, and provide an interesting fact about the character.
>
> * **Interviewee:** Pretend you are the character throughout the interview. Answer the questions as you imagine the character would answer them. You may also try to talk and act the way you imagine the character would.

FOUR CHARACTERS, ONE SCENE

Read the passage that ends Chapter 46 (pages 288–290). Although this is a very brief scene, it demonstrates the personalities and roles of the four characters in it. As you read, think about how this scene represents the relationships between the characters in the novel. Explain how each character's actions in this scene are typical of his or her characterization throughout the novel. Then give an example from a different part of the novel that also shows this characterization.

1. In this scene, Willow is _____

_____

_____

_____

▶ How does this behavior relate to Willow's character throughout the whole novel?

_____

_____

_____

▶ Find a quotation from a different passage that shows this characterization. Include page numbers.

_____

_____

2. In this scene, Mai is _____

_____

_____

_____

▶ How does this behavior relate to Mai's character throughout the whole novel?

_____

_____

_____

▶ Find a quotation from a different passage that shows this characterization. Include page numbers.

_____

_____

FOUR CHARACTERS, ONE SCENE (cont.)

3. In this scene, Dell is _____

_____

_____

▶ How does this behavior relate to Dell's character throughout the whole novel?

_____

_____

▶ Find a quotation from a different passage that shows this characterization. Include page numbers.

_____

_____

4. In this scene, Quang-ha is _____

_____

_____

▶ How does this behavior relate to Quang-ha's character throughout the novel?

_____

_____

▶ Find a quotation from a different passage that shows this characterization. Include page numbers.

_____

_____

5. In this scene, the group is _____

_____

_____

_____

▶ How does this behavior relate to how the group interacts throughout the novel?

_____

_____

_____

Name: _____

DYNAMIC HELPERS

A character can be *static* or *dynamic*. A *static character* does not change. For example, a story might have a loving and helpful parent who is exactly the same at the end of the book as she was at the beginning. This type of character is a *static character*. A *dynamic character* changes in some way. This type of character might start out as immature and selfish and change by the end of the story to become mature and thoughtful. Or a character might start out as a bully and eventually feel sorry for his actions and change his behavior.

Counting by 7s has both static and dynamic characters. In many novels, the protagonist is a dynamic character, and the way this character changes is connected to the theme of the novel. However, secondary characters can also be dynamic. Several of the characters in *Counting by 7s* change as a result of their relationship with Willow. Answer the questions about these characters and find evidence from the text to support your answers. Be sure to include page numbers for quotations.

Secondary Character: _____Dell Duke_____

	What is the character like at this point?	Character-revealing quotation from this section
Beginning of the novel		
Middle of the novel		
End of the novel		

1. Why do you think meeting Willow affects Dell this way?

_____

_____

_____

Name: _____

DYNAMIC HELPERS (cont.)

Secondary Character: ____Quang-ha____

	What is the character like at this point?	Character-revealing quotation from this section
Beginning of the novel		
Middle of the novel		
End of the novel		

2. Why do you think living with Willow changes Quang-ha?

_____

_____

Secondary Character: ____Jairo Hernandez____

	What is the character like at this point?	Character-revealing quotation from this section
Beginning of the novel		
Middle of the novel		
End of the novel		

3. Why do you think Jairo is so devoted to this girl he hardly knows?

_____

_____

On a separate sheet of paper, explain which character—Dell Duke, Quang-ha, or Jairo—you think changes the most in the novel, and why.

ANOTHER POINT OF VIEW

The author of *Counting by 7s* chose to alternate between first-person and third-person narration. Most chapters are narrated by Willow, but others are written in a third-person point of view and tell the readers about the thoughts and actions of all the characters.

1. Willow is a very unusual little girl. How does the author's choice to use first-person for Willow help you understand the character better than third-person would have?

    _____

    _____

    _____

    _____

Reread the scene (Chapter 45, page 271) in which Willow thanks the Nguyens and Dell during dinner. This chapter is narrated by Willow in first-person. Choose one of the other characters and write a paragraph from that person's point of view describing what that character thought and felt after Willow's statement.

Character's Name: _____

_____

_____

_____

_____

_____

_____

_____

2. What would this first-person paragraph add to the scene that could not be told through Willow's point of view?

    _____

    _____

    _____

    _____

SHARING POINTS OF VIEW

On the previous page, you wrote a paragraph from the first-person perspective of a character other than Willow. With your partner, discuss your paragraphs. One partner should read his or her paragraph first while the other listens, then switch roles.

Your Name: _____

Your Partner's Name: _____

What did you like best about your partner's version of the story? Do you agree with the way your partner interpreted the character's thoughts? Explain.

_____
_____
_____
_____

DISCUSS TOGETHER

Discuss the following questions and write down your answers.

1. Why do you think the author chose to include some third-person chapters rather than tell the whole story from Willow's point of view?

_____
_____
_____
_____

2. Could the novel have worked as well if the chapters were narrated in first-person by different characters? Explain.

_____
_____
_____

3. How do you feel about the story switching from one character's point of view to third-person point of view? Did it make the book harder to read or more interesting for you?

_____
_____
_____

Name: _____

I PREDICT

At the end of *Counting by 7s*, Willow gets to stay with her new family of friends. The book does not tell us what happens to Willow or the others in the years to come. Think about all of the characters and events in the book and make predictions about what will happen to the characters in the next year as Willow enters high school, Mai is a junior, and Quang-ha is a senior. Use quotations from the novel as evidence that shows why you made each prediction.

	Prediction	Quotation
Willow		
Mai		
Quang-ha		
Pattie		
Jairo		
Dell		

Name(s): _____

CREATE A NOVEL POSTER

Your group will work together to create a poster that represents one important chapter from *Counting by 7s*. Your teacher will assign your group one of these chapters.

Chapter 3	Chapter 8
Chapter 18	Chapter 28
Chapter 36	Chapter 41
Chapter 46	Chapter 60

Our group has been assigned Chapter _____.

Talk about the events in your chapter and decide which details are the most important to share.

Your poster should contain all of the following elements. Write down who will be in charge of each.

	Elements	Assigned to
1	▪ the number of the chapter ▪ a short explanation of what happens in this chapter (two or three sentences)	
2	▪ the point of view (Willow or third-person) ▪ a short explanation of the importance of this chapter to the overall plot	
3	▪ an image representing the most important event in this chapter ▪ a short description of the scene	
4	▪ an image that represents the setting of this event ▪ a one-sentence explanation of where the event takes place and phrases from the chapter that create a sense of place	
5	▪ word or words that represent the feeling or mood of this scene ▪ an explanation of why this mood is appropriate in the scene	
6	▪ a quotation from this scene ▪ a short explanation of the significance of the quotation	

TIPS:

❋ **Be creative!** You may draw pictures, use pictures from magazines, print images from the Internet (with permission from your teacher), or paste on objects that relate to the story.

❋ **Plan before you start.** Everyone should collect pictures and ideas before anyone begins writing on the poster board. Work together to design the look of the poster by placing all pictures before you paste them. Don't forget to leave room for the written parts.

UNIT 8 TEACHER INSTRUCTIONS

The worksheets in this section provide activities intended specifically to be used with the novel *All the Broken Pieces*.

Unit 8 includes the following components. See page 5 of this book for an explanation of icons.

 "Sum It Up!" (page 83) — Use focused practice opportunities to build summary skills. (*TIP:* If the novel is a read-aloud, stop at the designated page numbers and allow students to write their summaries. As a class, discuss which important events should be in each summary. If students are reading the novel on their own, have them complete the summaries for homework after they finish each of the designated sections.)

 "Changes" (pages 84–85) — Learn the difference between static and dynamic characters. Identify how Matt and Rob change and the effect each character has on the other.

 "Dynamic Discussion" (page 86) — With a partner, build on the previous activity. Discuss the significance of the changes in each character.

 "Getting to Know Secondary Characters" (page 87) — Work in pairs to analyze a secondary character and create an interview. Each team will role-play their character and interviewer in front of the class.

 "Transforming Form" (page 88) — Think about genre and point of view by rewriting a scene in prose rather than poetry and from the point of view of a different character. (*TIP:* After students complete the activity, have volunteers read their paragraphs. Discuss the differences between prose and poetry, and how form affects reading.)

 "Imagining Matt's Future" (page 89) — Review several poems in the novel and make predictions about the way the protagonist would likely continue to develop after the events in the novel. Examine how Matt responded to conflict and determine how the experience has changed him.

 "*All the Broken Pieces* Posters" (page 90) — As a group, create a poster that identifies poetic elements in one of the poems. (*TIP:* This activity should be used along with or after you have completed a poetry unit that introduces students to poetic devices. The poems used in this activity have been selected because they contain examples of poetic devices such as simile, symbolism, imagery, and repetition.)

 "Conduct a Gallery Walk" (page 91) — Generate questions and discussion based on the posters created in the previous activity. (*TIP:* Hang the posters around the room and have each group walk around to each poster. Give them sticky notes on which to write questions for each poster. When all the groups have walked around the room and written questions, have each group read and answer the questions on their poster.)

 "Finding Out the Facts" (page 92) — Research topics about the Vietnam War to find more information about the events depicted or referenced in the novel. After taking notes on the factual information, reflect on the differences in reading factual and fictional accounts of real events.

 "Historical Events, Fictional Accounts" (page 93) — Share research from the "Finding the Facts" handout and work together to perform a close reading of a key scene in the novel. Practice speaking and listening skills by answering questions about how the author weaves fact and fiction into the novel.

Name: _____

SUM IT UP!

A **summary** is a short explanation of the main points of a longer work. To write a summary of a novel, use your own words to identify the major events that happen in the story. Include only the most important points. Do not include your opinion or reaction to the writing.

All the Broken Pieces is told through a series of poems rather than chapters. The poems are separated with lines but do not have titles. This activity will help you practice your summary skills and give you an opportunity to stop and process what is happening in the novel. After you finish reading each set of pages listed below, stop and write a brief summary of what happened in that section. Focus on explaining the important events, not small details.

Beginning (pages 1–69)

_____

_____

_____

_____

_____

Middle (pages 70–149)

_____

_____

_____

_____

_____

End (pages 150–220)

_____

_____

_____

_____

_____

_____

Name: _____

CHANGES

A character can be *static* or *dynamic*. A *static character* does not change, while a *dynamic character* changes in some way. *All the Broken Pieces* has both static and dynamic characters. Most of the adults in the book are static characters. They do not change. However, Matt and Rob do change in response to the events that happen in the novel.

Complete the chart below to describe each dynamic character's behavior and attitude during the following scenes. Include quotations to support your answers.

	Matt	Rob
Tryouts		
Quotation to support your answer:		
The start of baseball season		
Quotation to support your answer:		

1. When Matt attends baseball tryouts, he does not seem happy about the prospect of being on the team. Why do you think he tried out for the baseball team and stayed on it despite his feelings? Include a quotation that supports your answer.

_____

_____

_____

_____

_____

Name: _____

CHANGES (cont.)

Expand the chart you began on the previous page. Describe each dynamic character's behavior and attitude during these scenes. Include quotations to support your answers.

	Matt	Rob
Chris as new coach		
Quotation to support your answer:		
The blindfold exercise		
Quotation to support your answer:		
End of the novel		
Quotation to support your answer:		

2. Look at pages 166–167. Before this point, Matt has not responded to the boys who bully him. Why do you think he finally speaks up here?

_____

_____

_____

_____

DYNAMIC DISCUSSION

With your partner, share your answers from the chart you completed on the previous pages. Use that information to discuss two of the most dynamic characters from *All the Broken Pieces*. Use the following questions to prompt a discussion about Matt and Rob.

PRACTICE SPEAKING AND LISTENING!

Take turns giving an opinion while the other person listens, paraphrases, and responds.

Speaker 1: _____   **Speaker 2:** _____
        (name)   *(name)*

Answer the following question aloud and support your opinion with examples from the novel. *How does Matt change after he tells his story to Rob and to his parents? What does he realize?*	Listen to Speaker 1's answer. Paraphrase your partner's claim. Then state whether or not you agree with your partner's opinion. Explain your position. ***then*** Answer the following question aloud and support your opinion with examples from the novel. *Why does Matt's story seem to change Rob? What does Rob realize?*
Listen to Speaker 2's answer. Paraphrase your partner's claim. Then state whether or not you agree with your partner's opinion. Explain your position.	

Discuss who you think changes the most in the novel, Matt or Rob. Each partner should take a different position and state evidence to prove why his or her character changed the most. Write each argument on the lines provided.

Here is why Matt changed the most over the course of *All the Broken Pieces*:

_____

_____

_____

_____

Here is why Rob changed the most over the course of *All the Broken Pieces*:

_____

_____

_____

_____

Name(s): _____

GETTING TO KNOW SECONDARY CHARACTERS

Matt is the main character in *All the Broken Pieces*, but the other characters are important, too. The secondary characters help readers understand the main character better and help move the plot along. You and a partner will analyze one secondary character and create a mock interview that demonstrates the character's personality.

Your teacher will assign one of these secondary characters to you and your partner.

Matt's adoptive mom	Coach Robeson	Rob
Matt's adoptive dad	Chris Williams	Alex
Matt's mother	Jeff	

Write your assigned character's name here: _____

You and your partner will present a live interview of your assigned character. One of you will pretend to be the character, and the other will be the interviewer. Work together to plan your interview. Write five questions you would like to ask your assigned character. Use questions that require more than a one-word answer. There are four question starters below to help you. Create your own question for #5.

1. Tell us about _____

2. What did you think when _____

3. How would you _____

4. Explain why _____

5. _____

Be prepared! Discuss how the character would answer these questions. Practice your presentation.

TIPS:

* **Interviewer:** Give the audience a brief introduction to the character, explain how the character knows Matt, and provide an interesting fact about the character.

* **Interviewee:** Pretend you are the character throughout the interview. Answer the questions as you imagine the character would answer them. You may also try to talk and act the way you imagine the character would.

Name: _____

TRANSFORMING FORM

All the Broken Pieces is a verse novel. The author tells Matt's story through free-verse poetry rather than prose. The novel still has a plot and characters like a prose novel, but the form of the novel is poetry. Reread the poems on pages 87–91 about Jeff and Matt's experience in the diner.

Imagine you are Jeff. Rewrite this scene as a prose paragraph from Jeff's point of view. Jeff does not know what Matt is thinking about, but what thoughts might Jeff have during this scene? Using first-person, describe what happened and what Jeff was seeing and thinking. Use additional paper or the back of the worksheet if you need more space.

_____
_____
_____
_____
_____
_____
_____
_____
_____
_____

1. What are the differences between your prose version and the original poem?

_____
_____
_____

2. Does poetry fit the character and the story better than prose? Why or why not?

_____
_____
_____

3. How would presenting the story through prose change the way you read the novel?

_____
_____
_____

Name: _____

IMAGING MATT'S FUTURE

At the end of *All the Broken Pieces*, a lot has changed for Matt. The book ends on a hopeful note, though it does not tell the readers what will happen in the future. Consider how Matt's character develops, and use this to make predictions about the character's future.

1. Reread the poem on page 69. Matt's adoptive parents tell him they love him all the time, but Matt is constantly worried that they won't want him anymore. Explain at least one reason why Matt feels so insecure about his parents' love.

   _____

   _____

   _____

   Find a quotation from another poem to support your answer. Include the page number.

   _____

   _____

   _____

2. Reread the poem on pages 207–208, paying close attention to Matt's mother's words. Explain what Matt's adoptive mother means and why she says this to Matt.

   _____

   _____

   _____

3. How do you think Matt's relationship with his adoptive parents will change?

   _____

   _____

   _____

4. Although Matt is a very talented pitcher, he does not seem to enjoy being on the baseball team throughout most of the novel. Reread the poems on pages 210–211. Do you think Matt will try out for the baseball team again in 8th grade? Why or why not?

   _____

   _____

   _____

Use the back of this worksheet or a separate sheet of paper to write a paragraph describing what you think Matt's 8th-grade year will be like. What will be different at school and on the baseball team? How will Matt be different? Will some things be the same?

ALL THE BROKEN PIECES *POSTERS*

Your group will work together to create a poster that analyzes one important poem from *All the Broken Pieces.* Your teacher will assign your group one of the following poems (indicated by page numbers).

page 2	pages 11–12	page 87	pages 168–169
page 8	pages 17–18	page 115	page 198

Our group has been assigned the poem on page(s) _____.

First, your group should read the poem aloud so you can hear the sound of the language. One person may volunteer to read the entire poem, or several members may take turns reading a few lines each.

Discuss the poetic elements and main idea of the poem. Take notes on your discussion. As a group, create a poster based on your poem. Your poster should contain all of the following elements. Write down who will be in charge of each.

	Elements	Assigned to
1	▪ the page number(s) of the poem ▪ a short explanation of the context of the poem and how its subject relates to the rest of the plot	
2	▪ pictures or graphics to represent ideas, images, and tone of the poem ▪ the main idea of the poem	
3	▪ an image representing the most important event in the poem ▪ a short description of the scene	
4	▪ several examples of figurative language (similes, metaphors, hyperbole, personification, symbols) used in the poem	
5	▪ several examples of sound devices (repetition, alliteration, consonance, onomatopoeia, assonance) used in the poem	
6	▪ several examples of word choice (connotations, sensory imagery, tone) used in the poem	

TIPS:

✳ **Be creative!** You may draw pictures, use pictures from magazines, print images from the Internet (with permission from your teacher), or paste on objects that relate to the story.

✳ **Plan before you start.** Everyone should collect pictures and ideas before anyone begins writing on the poster board. Work together to design the look of the poster by placing all pictures before you paste them. Don't forget to leave room for the written parts.

Name(s): _____

CONDUCT A GALLERY WALK

Each group in your class has created a poster, and now these posters are on display. As a group, walk around your classroom and take a look at the posters created by the other groups. This is your chance to ask questions about each group's choices. It will also be your chance to answer questions about the choices you made when creating your group's poster.

Consider the following ideas when writing questions about other groups' posters:

Is an idea on the poster not clear?

Do you disagree with a point the poster makes?

Do you want more information about something the group has included?

Do you want to ask how the group felt about any particular scene or character?

Do you want to bring up something you thought was important in that section that isn't included on the poster?

Name: _____

FINDING OUT THE FACTS

All the Broken Pieces is a work of historical fiction that is set in the late 1970s. Although the story is fiction, real historical events are important to the plot of the novel. The author depicts the Vietnam War, the treatment of returning Vietnam veterans, and the experience of refugee children in Matt's story.

Select one of the topics below and do some research about it.

Treatment of Vietnam Veterans	**Agent Orange**
American Vietnam War babies	**Operation Babylift**

Find two sources about your chosen topic. For each one, name the source and explain what you learned from it.

Source 1: _____

What facts did you learn from this source?

_____

_____

_____

Source 2: _____

What facts did you learn from this source?

_____

_____

_____

How did reading about the Vietnam War in these sources differ from the experience of reading Matt's story in the novel?

_____

_____

_____

_____

Name(s): _____

HISTORICAL EVENTS, FICTIONAL ACCOUNTS

Share your research on the Vietnam War with your partner. After you discuss the facts you learned about the war, reread the poems on pages 153–161 of *All the Broken Pieces*. Pay close attention to the way the author uses facts from history to create this scene at the Veteran Voices meeting. Discuss what information from these poems seems like facts the author got through research. What imaginary details and descriptions does the author create to make the facts come to life?

Identify three pieces of information from this passage that probably came from research:

Information #1: _____

Why you believe the author obtained this from research: _____

_____

Information #2: _____

Why you believe the author obtained this from research: _____

_____

Information #3: _____

Why you believe the author obtained this from research: _____

_____

PRACTICE SPEAKING AND LISTENING!

Take turns giving an opinion while the other person listens, paraphrases, and responds.

Speaker 1: _____
(name)

Speaker 2: _____
(name)

Answer the following question aloud and support your opinion with reasoning. *Do you think the author did a good job capturing what this experience at the Veteran Voices meeting was like? Give an example.*	Listen to Speaker 1's answer. Paraphrase your partner's claim. **then** Answer the following question aloud and support your opinion with reasoning. *How can reading historical fiction novels help students understand history in a different way than reading articles or textbooks?*
Listen to Speaker 2's answer. Paraphrase your partner's claim.	

COMMON CORE CORRELATIONS

The lessons and activities included in *Using Paired Novels to Build Close Reading Skills, Grades 7–8* meet the following Common Core State Standards. (©Copyright 2010. National Governors Association Center for Best Practices and Council of Chief State School Officers. All rights reserved.) For more information about the Common Core State Standards, go to *http://www.corestandards.org/* or visit *http://www.teachercreated.com/standards/* for more correlations to Common Core State Standards. (**Note:** When the standards are the same or nearly the same for both grade levels, their descriptions are listed only once.)

Reading: Literature	
Key Ideas and Details	**Pages**
ELA.RL.7.1 Cite several pieces of textual evidence to support analysis of what the text says explicitly as well as inferences drawn from the text.	10, 12–14, 20, 22–23, 28, 31–32, 36–49, 53, 56, 60–61, 65, 70–71, 74–77, 80–81, 84–85, 89
ELA.RL.8.1 Cite the textual evidence that most strongly supports an analysis of what the text says explicitly as well as inferences drawn from the text.	10, 12–14, 20, 22–23, 28, 31–32, 36–49, 53, 56, 60–61, 65, 70–71, 74–77, 80–81, 84–85, 89
ELA.RL.7.2. / ELA.RL.8.2 Determine a theme or central idea of a text and analyze its development over the course of the text; provide an objective summary of the text.	10, 12–14, 19–25, 28–29, 36–49, 54–55, 65, 70–72, 74–75, 83–86, 89
ELA.RL.7.3 Analyze how particular elements of a story or drama interact (e.g., how setting shapes the characters or plot).	12, 14, 20–24, 28–31, 36–49, 53–61, 65, 70–79, 81, 84–90
ELA.RL.8.3 Analyze how particular lines of dialogue or incidents in a story or drama propel the action, reveal aspects of a character, or provoke a decision.	10, 12–15, 20–25, 28–29, 31, 36–49, 53–61, 65, 70–71, 73–79, 81, 84–90
Craft and Structure	**Pages**
ELA.RL.7.4. / ELA.RL.8.4 Determine the meaning of words and phrases as they are used in a text, including figurative and connotative meanings.	*all activity pages*
ELA.RL.8.5 Compare and contrast the structure of two or more texts and analyze how the differing structure of each text contributes to its meaning and style.	21, 24–25, 36–39, 56–57, 60–61
ELA.RL.7.6 Analyze how an author develops and contrasts the points of view of different characters or narrators in a text.	10, 12–15, 24, 38–49, 56–59, 71, 74–79, 84–86, 88
ELA.RL.8.6 Analyze how differences in the points of view of the characters and the audience or reader (e.g., created through the use of dramatic irony) create such effects as suspense or humor.	14, 38–43, 56–59, 73–79, 84–88

94

COMMON CORE CORRELATIONS (cont.)

Reading: Literature *(cont.)*	
Integration of Knowledge and Ideas	**Pages**
ELA.RL.7.9 Compare and contrast a fictional portrayal of a time, place, or character and a historical account of the same period as a means of understanding how authors of fiction use or alter history.	28–29, 92–93
Range of Reading and Level of Text Complexity	**Pages**
ELA.RL.8.10 By the end of the year, read and comprehend literature, including stories, dramas, and poems, in the grades 6–8 text complexity band independently and proficiently.	*all activity pages*

Writing	
Text Types and Purposes	**Pages**
ELA.W.7.1. / ELA.W.8.1. Write arguments to support claims with clear reasons and relevant evidence.	*all activity pages*
ELA.W.7.2. / ELA.W.8.2. Write informative/explanatory texts to examine a topic and convey ideas, concepts, and information through the selection, organization, and analysis of relevant content.	*all activity pages*
ELA.W.7.3. / ELA.W.8.3. Write narratives to develop real or imagined experiences or events using effective technique, relevant descriptive details, and well-structured event sequences.	66–67, 78
Production and Distribution of Writing	**Pages**
ELA.W.7.4. / ELA.W.8.4. Produce clear and coherent writing in which the development and organization are appropriate to task, purpose, and audience.	*all activity pages*
ELA.W.7.5. / ELA.W.8.5. With some guidance and support from peers and adults, develop and strengthen writing as needed by planning, revising, editing, rewriting, or trying a new approach, focusing on how well purpose and audience have been addressed.	45–49, 60–61, 67
Research to Build and Present Knowledge	**Pages**
ELA.W.7.8. / ELA.W.8.8. Gather relevant information from multiple print and digital sources.	*all activity pages*
ELA.W.7.9. / ELA.W.8.9. Draw evidence from literary or informational texts to support analysis, reflection, and research.	*all activity pages*
ELA.W.7.9A. Apply *grade 7 Reading standards* to literature (e.g., "Compare and contrast a fictional portrayal of a time, place, or character and a historical account of the same period as a means of understanding how authors of fiction use or alter history").	*all activity pages*
ELA.W.8.9A. Apply *grade 8 Reading standards* to literature (e.g., "Analyze how a modern work of fiction draws on themes, patterns of events, or character types from myths, traditional stories, or religious works such as the Bible, including describing how the material is rendered new").	*all activity pages*

Speaking and Listening	
Comprehension and Collaboration	**Pages**
ELA.SL.7.1. / ELA.SL.8.1. Engage effectively in a range of collaborative discussions (one-on-one, in groups, and teacher-led) with diverse partners on grade 7 [and grade 8] topics and texts, building on others' ideas and expressing their own clearly.	11, 15, 19, 21–22, 24, 29–30, 32, 36–37, 40, 53–54, 58–59, 71, 73, 79, 81, 86–87, 90–91, 93
ELA.SL.7.2. Analyze the main ideas and supporting details presented in diverse media and formats (e.g., visually, quantitatively, orally) and explain how the ideas clarify a topic, text, or issue under study.	15, 24, 30, 71, 86, 91
ELA.SL.7.3. / ELA.SL.8.3. Delineate a speaker's argument and specific claims, evaluating the soundness of the reasoning and relevance and sufficiency of the evidence and identifying when irrelevant evidence is introduced.	24, 30, 71, 86
Presentation of Knowledge and Ideas	**Pages**
ELA.SL.7.4. / ELA.SL.8.4. Present claims and findings, emphasizing salient points in a focused, coherent manner with relevant evidence, sound valid reasoning, and well-chosen details; use appropriate eye contact, adequate volume, and clear pronunciation.	36–37, 73, 81, 87, 90–91
ELA.SL.7.5. / ELA.SL.8.5. Integrate multimedia and visual displays into presentations to clarify information, strengthen claims and evidence, and add interest.	81, 90–91
ELA.SL.7.6. / ELA.SL.8.6. Adapt speech to a variety of contexts and tasks, demonstrating command of formal English when indicated or appropriate.	73, 81, 90–91

Language	
Conventions of Standard English	**Pages**
ELA.L.7.1. / ELA.L.8.1. Demonstrate command of the conventions of standard English grammar and usage when writing or speaking.	*all activity pages*
ELA.L.7.2. / ELA.L.8.2. Demonstrate command of the conventions of standard English capitalization, punctuation, and spelling when writing.	*all activity pages*
Knowledge of Language	**Pages**
ELA.L.7.3. / ELA.L.8.3. Use knowledge of language and its conventions when writing, speaking, reading, or listening.	*all activity pages*
ELA.L.7.4. / ELA.L.8.4. Determine or clarify the meaning of unknown and multiple-meaning words and phrases based on *grade 7 [and grade 8] reading and content*, choosing flexibly from a range of strategies.	*all activity pages*
Vocabulary Acquisition and Use	**Pages**
ELA.L.7.5. / ELA.L.8.5. Demonstrate understanding of figurative language, word relationships, and nuances in word meanings.	*all activity pages*
ELA.L.7.6. / ELA.L.8.6. Acquire and use accurately grade-appropriate general academic and domain-specific words and phrases; gather vocabulary knowledge when considering a word or phrase important to comprehension or expression.	*all activity pages*